Tales From the Third Floor

LINDA TODD

authorHOUSE®

AuthorHouse™
1663 Liberty Drive
Bloomington, IN 47403
www.authorhouse.com
Phone: 1-800-839-8640

First published by AuthorHouse 4/8/2010

ISBN: 978-1-4520-0342-9 (e)
ISBN: 978-1-4520-0343-6 (sc)

Library of Congress Control Number: 2010904136

Printed in the United States of America
Bloomington, Indiana

This book is printed on acid-free paper.

September 1, 1999 - Lions and tigers and bears, oh my.

Okay, here is the deal. Last night Mom went to sleep fine, but this morning at about 5:30 I came upstairs, and all the lights were on, and stuff was moved around, the hamster cage was opened, and the hamster was gone. I didn't see him anywhere. I looked in Mom's room, and she was sound asleep. I was a little scared I can tell you. I thought maybe she had eaten the poor little guy, she hates it . So, about 7:00 she comes up the stairs, her pants are on backward, and she had some strange concoction of shirts on, and she's saying, "There is some animal flying around my room, and I can't catch him, and it's really bothering me." I am cracking up just writing it.

Dad still seems confused, he thought the kids were making a lot of turkey sandwiches today. One each, but I guess that was a lot to him. He had a good night. Mom is a bit out of it today, roaming around with flying animals and such. By the way, she hadn't eaten him, we found him.

September 2, 1999 - The operative word being testy.

Mom was testy last night, I think Dad makes her testy. I feel so bad for both of them. She was very confused about where their bed was yesterday and kept asking Dad over and over where it was, and he was being just as impatient and testy as he could be. I couldn't figure out why he was being so impatient until he said that "she" was talking about the bed. I asked if he thought she was thinking about sex, and he said, "Yes." I said, "Dad, she's just confused about where the beds are. It was hard for Mom when you were in the hospital. She isn't thinking about sex." So, he relaxed and then was nice to her. She had her feelings hurt and didn't know why he was so mad at her. I just want to cry. Yesterday he sat at the table and said, "I am not worth anything anymore." All I could say is, "Your worth doesn't have anything to do with what you can do, Dad, it just is because you are." Does that sound wise? I just wish he would be nice to her more consistently instead of being so scared.

September 3, 1999

Mom is signed up to go September 15th for her first day of daycare. Dad is already thinking that she should go two days instead of one, but we will take it a step at a time. Love you

September 8, 1999 - Storms inside and out.

It was such a long day yesterday, I didn't think it would ever end, and it sure ended with a bang, a huge lightning storm with thunder and rain. It was wonderful and just exactly how I felt inside, stormy and suffocated. I was having such a hard time with all the things I had to do that it was all I could do to maintain, and I did not do that very well.

All the phone calls and paperwork that are involved with getting some home health care started are daunting to me. Susan or George, will you call me so I can tell you what I need?

Last night I had an appointment with Fr. Fink, and I am so glad that it was yesterday. We had a nice spiritual chat. Today proves to be much happier. I feel better, and I will have a little reprieve today when Mom and Dad go with their friends. Fall is in the air, and that always lifts my spirits.

I wish the folks would enjoy this computer stuff. Right now they are sitting and watching me, waiting. Dad is waiting to poop, Mom wonders if she has to go to work, and Dad didn't sleep last night because of the storm. Dear, dear me…I love you all.

September 9, 1999

They had a wonderful time with their friends yesterday. It was a nice break for me, and it sounded like Mom did just fine at lunch. Stan and Edna were surprised at the change in Mom, as I expected they would be. I cried yesterday on the way to somewhere because I have been so full of myself with lots of self pity and with feeling suffocated, but the tears were a release. So, today is a happy and hopeful day just in time for my birthday. Mom didn't really remember it, but Dad did, and I was pleased at that, and he also started the happy birthday song. Mom doesn't remember anything about yesterday's visit at all, nor who Stan and Edna are.

I went to a seminar on Alzheimer's last night. It was a two hour general overview but very informative and interesting. Mom gets irritable in the evening and often doesn't eat and crabs around, but now I know there is a name for that, it's called sundowning. They spend a lot of energy trying to cope in the day, and at night they just crash. Also the following around she does is called shadowing, and everyone in the group felt the same kind of suffocation and smothering and invasion of personal space that I have been feeling by two because Dad does some of it as well, just for a different reason. I must have looked forlorn because the lady who was leading the group said I could call her whenever I wanted. I figured out something though. Mom crowds me a lot, and lately I have been asking her if she wants to go with me on quick runs. She usually ends up going, and that seems to be enough for her.

Then she leaves me alone in the house for a bit. It's working...
at least for now.

September 11, 1999

Last night Mom went to bed with her clothes on right after dinner. Mom hasn't been eating for the last few nights, and I noticed when I gave her a bath that her ribs are showing in her back, and she was already a little thin. So, I kept saying that she had to eat at night, and with some prodding she did and then went to bed. I went down to check on her, and as she lay there and talked, she suddenly sat up and said, "How are you doing?" Poor Mom, she wants so badly to be able to be a part of communicating and just can't very well, but we did talk and had a nice quiet time for about 15 minutes. Before that, when she was still upstairs, she asked if they were going to sleep with the dog (what dog?), and I said, "No." And then she said, "Norm, then I can climb up on you?" Of course, Dad got scared and said, "No," in his intimidating voice. So, I said, "Dad, I think Mom means that she wants to sleep next to you." She nodded. She had gotten her feelings hurt again and couldn't understand what she had said that was wrong.

It is foggy here today and lovely. It is pretty cool here too lately, very Fall-ish.

September 12, 1999

Here I was taking everyone to Don's brother's wedding, which was about an hour's drive away in the country, it was a lovely drive, by the way. Mom was riding in the front seat, and when we finally found it, she said that she was not going in. Before Dad could get a word in, I said that that was fine. So, we parked very close to the door of the place to make Dad feel more comfortable, and after assuring him that we would check on her every 15 minutes, he relented and came in with us. We went through the whole wedding with one of us checking on Mom, and each time she said, "No, I don't want to go in." Once the wedding was over, Dad went out and told her that they were going to be serving some food, and sure enough, she was ready to come in then and eat. She ended up having a great time because Don's family is very friendly and affectionate, and besides, one of the aunts has Alzheimer's, and the two of them kept each other company being silly and cute. Mom did fine and kept eating the peanuts after she said she didn't want any. We all had a good time.

September 13, 1999

Yesterday Mom hit Dad with her fist in his chest twice. She said he wasn't telling her the truth about not having a home to go to. She said, "I'm going to get you." I know, hide the knives, right? She continues to be very childlike to the point that she comes up and pulls your shirt up and then tickles you and laughs and says, "Gotcha," and truly expects you to tickle her back, which I sometimes do. Or she waves at you from across the room like we did when we were in grade school waving to a friend. It's such a role reversal that I am having trouble getting accustomed to this part. She still tries to do dishes, which is no small irritation to me, because it just means more work.

Yesterday, I spent most of the day praying for patience and perseverance, my attitude was the pits.

Her eating habits are most disconcerting at times. She takes huge chunks of food and sits way away from the table so she can't possibly eat well or without making a mess. She tries so hard that it is a very sad thing to watch. She takes her pills in the morning and doesn't swallow them because I think the vitamin is too large, so she ends up spitting them out. I have deleted the vitamin so she only has three small pills, and they went down easily this morning.

Last night when I was talking to Don in our room, Mom suddenly walked in and said, "What are you doing in there? This is your room, and you are in the right room." Dad was right behind her peeking in saying, "Thank you for everything." She said that she looked upstairs, and there was no one there, and she was looking for everyone. They left and supposedly went back to bed, but then a minute later she came out in the hall and said that the light was on upstairs and to go turn it off, (once a Mom, always a Mom). I said, "Mom, I'm going back upstairs to do something, I will turn it off later." She got mad and walked away muttering to herself. Dad was busy following her and saying, "Thank you for everything."

September 14, 1999

Today Dad had a headache, and they were both tired and dozed a lot, probably worried about tomorrow and the first daycare day. Yesterday when Dad was helping Mom into the van, she couldn't figure out how to move her legs to get in, and then when he was helping her out, she got mad and pushed him in the chest and said, "Get away." He almost fell. She seems to be mean to him lately, not to me or anyone else. She gets angry, and then in the next instant she says, "You're wonderful." She didn't eat tonight and was very confused this morning at breakfast. She put her pills in her bowl, then put water in with the bananas, and then poured the water out, then ate only a little. Who knows if she even got them? This could be a problem, ya think?

September 18, 1999 - Lunch tales.

Don took Mom and Dad to lunch today. Mom kept putting her big plate on a small plate, they finally got that one straightened out. Then she proceeded to eat the entire pieces of shrimp without taking the hard tails off, and didn't want the tails taken off. Then Don said that Mom said she didn't want any dessert, but Dad wanted some, and so they brought Don and Dad one, and Mom started eating Dad's. When Dad stuck his fork in his pie, she said, "What are you doing?" She pulled the plate away from him, whereupon Don gave Dad the rest of his. I guess Dad was looking quite forlorn about this time. Then Mom had sticky stuff on her fingers, so she stuck her fingers in her glass of water, but that didn't fix it, so she stuck her fingers in Dad's lemonade. During lunch Don said Mom was talking about how she had driven the other day and a policeman stopped her and asked her if she knew where she was going. Don just shook his head, but they all still had a good time.

Mom and I took a short walk, and there is this tree with red berries on it, which, of course, she noticed and took two of right away. And as I am saying, "Mom, they might be poisonous," she popped them into her mouth. Fortunately they were sour, and she spit them out quickly. Got to watch that.

September 20, 1999

Yesterday I said, "Mom, what do you think about when you're quiet?" After a minute or two she said, pointing to the pictures on the wall, "I think of the pictures being a family."

I asked her if she remembered how to sing any of the Pirates and Penzance, and she started to hum at first, then a few words from one of the songs came, and then suddenly she was remembering whole verses. She was so pleased with herself, and I could see the joy in her face. It made me happy, too, to hear her sing again.

Last night she came upstairs, and I asked her what she was doing. She said, "I DON'T KNOW, but I don't like the group there." The group was Jay and Donny and me. We are now the group.

And last night Dad was urinating blood, hmm, and Mom had an accident on her nightgown. So, today I have bloody undies, poopie nighties, and I have the runs. Not a good start … Help, Lord!!

Mom no longer knows how to brush her teeth. So, I take her downstairs to her bathroom, put the paste on it and give it to her, and then she can do it herself. Don't panic, these are the facts. Perhaps I am too close to see if she is doing well or not.

September 20, 1999

So, today while Dad is at the ER to have his bladder checked, Mom is busy looking out the window asking, "Where is Norm?" Often. I went upstairs and about 10 minutes later up she came with nylons on and Dad's sweater on, nothing else. When Dad is not here she is disoriented and agitated, but if I keep her busy and upstairs with us she seems calmer. I believe there is so much more to this disease than I could ever imagine. One needs to have a lot of imagination.

September 22, 1999 - Can I say overwhelmed?

I am overwhelmed with what a struggle it is to have to make decisions for Mom and Dad. Often lately the things that I am called upon to do are way outside of my experience and abilities. The decision to get Mom a pill to sedate her a bit one may think is easy, but in reality it is not. The knowledge that we need to do something is one thing, but the actual giving it to her and watching how it affects her, slows her down, makes her groggy and dopey, are so hard. I am always afraid that if she has too much in her system that she might not wake up, it is quite an overwhelming thing. Have I said it enough to make sure you know it's overwhelming?

September 23, 1999

Dad has had his Cystoscopy and medically is just fine. However, the build up of the medicines in his body for pain have had an adverse effect on him mentally. He was running about the halls in the hospital, gown flying, dragging his IV, looking about for what or whom? He has decided that I am out to get him, and that I keep changing his room to move him into a home somewhere. Hmm…he might have a thought. Just kidding. He has told George that I tie him up at home. Actually, these kinds of things do hurt, they do affect me. I know it is the medicine talking, and once it is out of his system he will return to his jovial, funny self, but in the meantime this is sad to me.

September 30, 1999 - The shoe box.

Yesterday went relatively well until Mom got hold of Dad's shoebox that was full of all his important papers. He had been working on it all morning until Mom suddenly said, "Get your papers out of here." She scooped them up and shoved them all in the shoebox. He was devastated and said, "She's nutty." He was beside himself. He must have stayed mad at her because she kept coming upstairs and roaming around and then going down again.

The afternoon was still more bizarre. She kept up the roaming and kept coming out with these bizarre words, and don't tell anyone else, but sometimes I knew what she was saying, eek.

The evening brought still more strangeness. They went to bed early, at least Dad did, and Mom kept coming up, and I would say, "Where is Dad?" And she would say, "I don't know, I'm looking for him." We would go downstairs, and I would say, "Mom, he's here in bed." He was ignoring her, I guess, waiting for someone to put her to bed. So I dressed her, well sort of, she wouldn't take her nylons off but, as she would say, "So what."

October 10,1999

Yesterday Mom was doing her roaming thing in the kitchen and telling everyone who was available that she is tired and asking what this thing or that thing was doing here. I said, "Mom, you're roaming, what are you looking for?" She said, "I'm looking for love." And I said, "Oh, I love you" and she replied, "I'm looking for a kiss from him," pointing at Dad, who, of course, sits there like a stone. So, she said, "But he won't give me one." So, when she walked out of the room, I asked Dad if he gave her a kiss, and he said, "No." So, I said, "Why don't you, and then she'll stop looking for one?" Oh, dear, it's like dealing with little kids.

October 11,1999

This morning the visiting lady from Catholic Charities came to sit with Mom for a while. Mom did her usual leave me alone thing and got up and walked outside. The lady and I sat and talked for a bit, and when Mom came back in, she was fine as if nothing had gone on before. She sat down and then enjoyed a couple hour visit.

She is like that with her pills too. She came up for breakfast this morning, put her pills in her water, then tried to put the cereal into the cup of water with the pills. I finally said, "Let's start over again, Mom." We did, and then she did just fine. Most of the time the starting over thing works. She got mad though when I didn't say I needed help with the lunch. It is so trying, that part of it. Dad is very helpful today and seems in much better spirits.

Susan, I am looking forward to coming out there, and the fare was only $192. Pretty good, huh? I think I fly on the back of a big bird, but, oh well.

October 12, 1999

Hi all,

Today the start over thing wasn't even necessary. Mom got up, and though tired, was smiling! Dad had trouble dressing her. She doesn't really care about wearing underwear, and that is fine with Dad because he doesn't know how to put them on her anyway. This morning I washed her hair, and then she went with me to pick up the kids. When we got home, I said, "Okay, Mom, we are home," to which she answered "No, we're still driving." But as she got out she said, "I am going to tell Dad." She was mad about something, who knows what, and so she said that he, Dad, wasn't going with the ladies again, and I said, "Well, I'm glad that you came with me," to which she answered, "Well, I'm not." It was a typical strange conversation.

My kids are having friend troubles, Susan, you are having friend troubles, I think we should all just stop having friend troubles..

October 12, 1999 - Scary bathroom stuff.

Just had to write this one. Tonight Dad was in the bathroom, and Mom said to me, "Dad wants you to do something in the bathroom." I said, "What?" She said, "I don't know, he just wants you to do something for him." S-L-O-W-L-Y I went to the door and said, "Dad, ahem, do you want me for something?" He said, "I need my pajamas, I forgot them." Phew.

October 13, 1999

This morning Dad got up early before Mom, and because he was hungry, he told Mom that he was up, and that he would see her upstairs. Pretty soon we heard some rustling, a toilet flush, and then shortly after I went to check on her, and she had Dad's slacks on and nothing else. Can you see me shaking my head? So, we put some good clothes on, and then up she came and got mad when she saw Dad and promptly refused to eat.

The Home Health Care agency called today, and they will let us know about coming out and helping. Oops, right now Mom is talking about church, and will I care if they die, and they don't live here at all.

I am trying to remember to pray as often as I am annoyed or frustrated. The Lord knows when and where the help will come from. I reminded Dad that Home Health Care called, and he said, "Yeah, I need help." Yep!

October 15, 1999

I didn't give Mom the Ativan today but will give it to her tonight. Dad is tired and has already had two walks. Yesterday at dinner Mom was busy pushing her plate all over the table. Don, who already had had a bad day, said, "Laura Mae, if you don't want your food, that's fine, but stop trying to push it all over the place." She got quiet then and refused to eat. She won't let me wash her hair, it has been three days, and she won't let me bathe her lately. I thought about this all last night, and I hope you all will agree with me that we should try the senior adult daycare one day a week. Home Health will take months to start, and I think Dad and I do need a breather at least one day a week. I spoke to Dad and said I wasn't trying to take the decision away from him, but that this is what we need to do, and his response was that he needed to have someone make the decision because he could not do it.

October 19, 1999

Mom stays very close to whoever she is near and wants to hold your hand. She is so fragile in spirit but still strong and wiry physically, what a contradiction. When she goes out to walk, she refuses to wear a coat, and then Dad goes to rescue her, and she is always so happy that he comes.

The visiting lady came today, and she and Mom stayed downstairs talking. All of a sudden Mom comes up and throws a bloody Kleenex at Donny, who was doing his homework. She apparently had fallen, and since her skin is paper thin, it just bled and bled. She says her backside hurts a lot, so perhaps a doctor's visit is in order. Donny definitely did not like the bloody Kleenex thing.

October 21, 1999

Mom had trouble getting up this morning so we got an appointment with the doctor because she was hurting. The appointment was fine, and there are no broken bones, thank the Lord! When the doctor asked what happened, she said in a very matter of fact voice, "She pushed me," the "she" meaning me. Uh-oh, I did not have a good feeling about this at all. He left the room and came back with someone whom I am sure was there to observe. And then, of course, I felt like I had to pass this "test" and was a complete dork. When we came home, I suggested she go downstairs and rest since we didn't want to exacerbate the pain by going up and down the stairs. Mom said, "No, I don't want an exasperation either," then she started to giggle, which, of course, made me giggle.

October 24, 1999

Sooooooo, Mom has this cough thing that Dad says makes her vomit once a day. She doesn't, but I guess to him it sounds like it. I think the cough center in her brain is being affected. Just call me Dr. Linda.

Still no social worker arresting me for elder abuse or anything, one more day of freedom.

I went to the senior residence thing today. I liked it. They have lots of things for them to do, and they will pair Mom with another lady who lives there, and, of course, meals are included. The suggestion was that I should not bring Dad at first, and I thought that was a very sound idea! They talked quite a bit about not arguing with Mom about things she says and that we should try to find out what age she is remembering and perhaps some conversation will follow. I will try. I wasn't arguing with her and trying to correct her but a little leery about entering her "world"....SCARY.

One of the things she asked of me was if I had a support group. I told her that my husband, my family, sister, brother and sister-in-law were my main support group, along with all the other family and friends I was writing to. Right now, you guys, you are it, and I think you are doing a great job!!

October 25, 1999

Update today is Mom is like the little girl with the spit curl in the middle of her head or something like that. She refused to put on her under things again and kept eyeing them as if they were demons. She tried to take Dad's pills, sat in his chair, he was beside himself. Her hand that she had skinned is very swollen. The nurse across the street came over and showed me what to do, the whole time Mom is saying, "So what, so what so what." Dad whispered to me later, "She is just being bitchy." Yep, you got it, Dad.

October 26, 1999

I was sad because Donny flunked his driver's test today. And then I was sad taking Mom to the daycare center and leaving her there. She did well though. I walked about with her for a bit. She stuck close to me until we saw the aviary. As we were looking at it I said goodbye and left, got in the van and cried. She looked so forlorn and vulnerable and confused. Been doing a lot of praying lately.

Oh, my gosh, must tell you the latest breakfast fiasco. I walked upstairs, and they were sitting at the table. Mom had bacon on top of her cereal and ate it all up. I looked at Dad, who raised his eyebrows. I almost cracked up. Later he said, "She took four pieces of bacon and cut them on top of the cereal, with bananas too." He didn't get any, he didn't like that, so he had three pieces of toast. While all this was going on, she was complaining that her leg hurt, and Dad was trying to put the heating pad on it, and she kept refusing. I finally asked, "Where does your leg hurt?" She said, "I'm not telling you because then he says I have to sit down."

She said an amazing thing tonight. "If I look sad, I'm not, I like to live."

October 28, 1999- Captain and old farmers.

So, yesterday it was the Captain Crunch, bacon and bananas thing. Today it's the taking a walk with Mom thing. I asked where Dad was, and she said, "He walked in one of these houses here," and then said, "he's an old farmer." Apparently old farmers just go in any house.

Lots of inappropriate food related behavior lately. Tonight she put her coleslaw in her Minestrone soup, except the soup went onto the plate with the coleslaw.

Afterwards, she went downstairs and started brushing her teeth. I thought, oh, good, she is doing it herself, and when I went to check, I saw that she was brushing it with Groom and Clean. Just want you to know that that was not fun trying to get <u>that</u> out of her mouth.

Dad says he thinks three or four days at the daycare center would be good. You have no idea, I am either cracking up or praying.

October 29, 1999- It's all in the interpretation.

Don took us out to pizza, and Mom immediately grabbed three pieces. Then before she was through with them, she took several more and ate them all. Dad is learning to keep eating while he is talking, especially with Donny and Jay at the table. If he stops eating to talk, the food may be gone, and he might not get a second helping. He doesn't sit on etiquette anymore, and he usually has two pieces of pie right away because he figured out that it may not be around the next day. However, here is the thing. Before we left for pizza, Mom decided to go sit in the van. About 10 minutes later, Dad, feeling sorry for her, went out there with her. I could see they were just sitting there saying nothing. So, finally, I went out there and sat for about 20 minutes, and we all just visited, well, if you could call it that. When I jumped in the van, Mom said, "Oh, how nice to see you," as if that is where they lived or something. You know, I am really beginning to understand her weird sentences and what she is trying to say, I am the interpreter right now.

I asked Mom today where she lives and she said, "Valpo, and I need to get back home to my mom." Dad gets so upset when she says things like that about where she wishes she were. Even when I use logic and say things like, you could no longer take care of her yourself, you were making yourself sick, it helps for a few days, and then it seems like he gets angry with himself again.

So, that is it for today. Mom has no idea where she is, and Dad has no idea what to do with his life.

Oh, Dad said he had a sitz bath today. I would like to know where THAT occurred, and therefore, he felt he didn't need a bath.

October 31, 1999

What a morning. Okay. So, first everyone was up and forgot the time change. So, we all decided to go to breakfast. Donny orders a sweet roll that comes with lots of butter on top that apparently looks to Donny like frosting. He takes a huge bite and is immediately grossed out with this huge wad of butter in his mouth. Jay was worried about the juice he ordered, and Dad was busy trying to find out what was wrong with the juice.

Laura is busy being nervous about her first choir concert. Mom decided to comb her own hair and then wash her face and her hair with Noxzema. Dad didn't comb his hair today, he was just exhausted.

November 3, 1999

Daycare is going well. Mom even did a one finger piano playing there. At home Dad kept his hat and coat on all day. When asked why, he said he wanted to make sure his head didn't almost get cold. When we picked Mom up, she remembered nothing and never eats. Even though she eats a lot of food there, in her mind they never feed her. Mom helped me by drying the dishes. She put everything in one cabinet, but at least they were dry. She dropped a spoon on the floor and yelled out a great big "Shit." I said, "Mom, remember patience." She said, "My mom said I could say that, and she taught me how to." O-kay!

Mom told Dad yesterday that she didn't know what his link was, and that she was following him at the place yesterday and wasn't telling him that she was there, but she doesn't know his link. He just looked at her and had no idea what to answer, and so we all just laughed because I was mystified. Most of the time I am mystified.

Laura was sitting at the computer, and suddenly she comes in gagging and says, "Grandpa's teeth are coming out of his head." When I went and looked, they were fine, he must have pushed them back in. But about 10 minutes later back in she comes saying the same thing. If you all only knew, it's like a zoo.

Much love on this lovely almost Lord's day.

November 7, 1999

We just came home from church, and the house smells like something is burning. Mom or Dad turned the oven temperature up to broil. So, it charred the pans that were in the oven and heated up the house pretty nicely. Scary, very scary. It smelled for several hours. Thank the Lord we were not staying away all day.

November 8, 1999

Sometimes I wish I could remember all the funny things Mom says. Like this one: Dad was in the living room, and Mom was in the kitchen waiting for dinner when she looked at Dad and said, "I better go sit with him." I said, "Why?" She said, "Cause he is such an old thing." One sentence sounds just fine, but the follow-up makes no sense. Sometimes when I remind her about being patient, she will say, "I don't like patience, it's dumb."

Tonight I asked Mom if she wanted to brush her teeth and she said, "No, I like my teeth this way." Hmm.

Mom was actually hungry tonight and then complimented me on my cooking. I will have to remake this dinner for sure.

November 9, 1999

Here's my day: I take Mom to the doctor, pick up Laura, go back to the doctor, then take Mom to daycare, then take Donny to his one class at school, then take Dad to the community center, then take Laura again, then pick them both up, and then I am done with the dropping off until I pick up Mom from the daycare.

Life is ever interesting. I can feel Mom and Dad's eyes boring into my back. Pretty funny.

November 10, 1999

Mom is on Celexa now, and it seems to be helping her with her combativeness. Today Dad's lip was swollen and infected. He didn't want to talk about it or go to the doctor. I think he's afraid they will put him in the hospital, and I'll tie him up again. I'll watch his lip.

Dad said today, "Linda, I know we are such a bother." I said, "No, you aren't," and I meant it. My attitude can be less than charitable at times, but they are not a bother, hard at times, yes, but worth it. I hope that I will not be a bother either when I am old and cranky and frail. I felt very humbled in my heart.

Mom seems to hide out in the van a lot. I hope that stops, it is cold out there, and one of us is always having to go out to check on her. She is having struggles with taking her pills again. Comes and goes.

Love you.

November 13, 1999

Dad had an accident today as he was running for the bathroom. He was trying to clean it up as best he could and didn't want me to help him. I am certain he was just embarrassed. I helped anyway, and together we got it cleaned up. Poor Dad, what a trial for him. He seems to be fine now. Where was Mom during all this? She was still in the van. She refused to come out, and no amount of logic would work. I told her that it was cold out, and that she should come in where it's warm. She said, "Well, that's what you do." She stayed there for about an hour.

November 15, 1999

Mom started being stubborn, angry and sad at about 2:00 today, and it lasted till she went to bed. She refused to eat dinner or drink anything, threw her glass of soda on the floor. She talked about dying and no one loving her, and she didn't like Dad, and he didn't love her, and she was just a burden, and on and on, and always getting back to the dying thing. I took her mind off of it by talking about memories from Valparaiso, which are always very dear to her, but then we were back on the whole dying bit. Then she would cry.

She refused to change her clothes to go to bed, so she went to sleep in her clothes. I guess you fight about the things that are most important, that one isn't. Anyway I am going to bed. Love to you all.

November 30, 1999

I am back from a lovely visit in California. And then Gina and the kids were here for about 10 days. We all had such a wonderful and often crazy time. Five extra people and lots more noise. Thankfully, Mom and Dad could go downstairs and close the door. Mom was just okay.

December 20, 1999

Mom cracked her pelvis about five days ago, from a fall. She is now in a rehab nursing home for a few weeks. The intake went well, but as it turns out, shortly after we left, whoever was supposed to watch Mom, didn't, and since she couldn't hold her own weight, she tried to get up and promptly fell. The whole of her face is puffed up, already two black eyes are showing, and there's a huge bump on her forehead. They had to call us to come out there. I was not pleased at all.

The next day they called to see if I would come and get her to eat. When I got there, she was sitting all alone at a table with the food in front of her and crying silently. Her hands were dirty, and she was slumped over the table. Oh, my gosh, the tears were so present, and honestly my heart felt crushed. I got a warm washcloth and soap and washed her hands, then washed her face, and talked to her quietly and fed her a few bites. She kept staring down while the tears dropped quietly on her hands in front of her.

A couple of days later she was having diarrhea, and they called again. When I went there I could see huge bruises on the back of her legs. She was actually scared and so glad to see me. I had them take her to the hospital to be assessed, knowing that she would NOT go back there! Jay went to the hospital with us, and she hung on to him for dear life. She will come back home, and we will take care of her and learn how to use the belt so that we can help her walk until her pelvis heals. Nursing homes are NOT all the same. Are you incensed? I am.

December 25, 1999 - A sort of Christmas letter.

This morning as I was listening to "Chestnuts Roasting on an Open Fire", I was reflecting on this Christmas season and how incredibly busy it has been, not just the usual busy but the busy-ness of taking care of parents who are aging and ill. My reflection took me all over the place, from self pity, to resignation, to acceptance, to joy...yes, even joy. I know that God's grace is sufficient, and when I am sane enough to leave it all in His hands, I am at peace, and when I don't, I am not. Simple. Hard. Important.

I am thankful for the support and encouragement you all give me too, and I am so glad that I can write all this to you, it helps, you have no idea.

Don and the kids are a never ending source of help, for which I am so grateful! Merry Christmas and a Happy New Year.

December 29, 1999

Mom is doing as well as can be expected physically, but she is laughing once in a while again. It is good to see and hear, and her mood is much better because of the medication she's on. This keeps her rages and depressions down to almost nothing. What she used to say she would never do, as in taking medications, is now the thing that holds her together just like glue.

The weather is beautiful today, and while she is healing, she has a wheelchair, and she likes being outside in it. She eats Kleenex, and so we give her handkerchiefs or napkins, cloth ones, to blow her nose and wipe her mouth. Dad keeps thinking that she can be fixed so she won't get upset and life would be easier. This makes me think of the times I get ornery and Don doesn't understand me, mea culpa.

Friends have said it is a blessing to be able to take care of my mother, and they are right. It is a role reversal and a difficult one, but if I am able to give any nurturing to this woman who nurtured me, Susan, and George, I say amen.

January 9, 2000

Mom decided to try and walk by herself. She held on to the bed, then the wall, then the bathroom door, and then fell. No real damage, but she cannot be left alone thinking she will remember that she cannot walk alone. Dad looked like he needed a break, so I went downstairs with her for awhile.

One morning, early, around 4:00 a.m., I was heading for the bathroom when I saw Mom and Dad crawling up the stairs. I said, "Dad, what are you doing?" He said, "We were hungry, and I know you said Mom can't walk by herself, so we decided to crawl upstairs." Oh, my gosh, I was just cracking up. I asked him why he didn't come and get me, and, of course, he didn't want to wake me up. When I asked him why he didn't put the belt on Mom's waist and walk her upstairs, he said he thought they would be safer crawling. By now he was laughing because I was laughing. I barely made it to the bathroom I was laughing so hard. They are such a pair! By the way, I got them back downstairs and got their cereal for them.

January 19, 2000 - Let it snow!

It is snowing and snowing and snowing finally, and it is beautiful!

Mom walked to the bathroom without any help except me walking beside her, hand ever ready to grab the belt that is around her waist. She is ever so much better!

January 20, 2000

My attitude is bleak today. I feel as if I am on call all the time, and even if I am not, I feel like any minute I will be. I notice that if I don't take time in the morning to pray, the day just spirals down, and I have to fight my way back up from the bottom of the well. I can't even think anymore tonight. I turned off the phone. I can't talk to another person tonight. I will call tomorrow if any of you called.

Tonight Mom was out of sorts with going to bed. I finally got her to lie down and covered her up, even though she was being stubborn, laying very still and stiff. I asked Dad if he was going to bed. He said, "Yes," and then proceeded to uncover Mom and mess the covers up. She was even staring at him like, what are you doing? "Whatcha doin, Dad?" says I , "are you going to bed?" He said, "Yes," again, and then went and sat down in the chair. I asked once more, and he got up and said, "Well, I can't get Mom bunched up." I can tell you that I have NO idea what the heck he is going to do next or for that matter what Mom is going to do next.

Susan, anybody, where are you? Are you all tired of my whining yet? I hope not too badly. I am feeling less put upon tonight, I just hope no one asks me to do anything. Love you.

January 27, 2000 - Socks, shoes and messes.

It has been several days as you can see. Where do I start? Mom pooped all over the rug and bathroom floor yesterday.

I just had walked in the door, and there it was. Dad kept stepping in it with his shoe, and then he took that off and stepped in it with his sock. In his confusion he just couldn't walk around or over it. It was hilariously funny and not funny at the same time. She kept saying that there was poop on the floor ….H-E-L-L-O…and that the bathroom was dirty. I got it all cleaned up, shoes, socks and bathroom, and then gave her a shower. Dad meanwhile walked around with one bare foot and the other with his sock and shoe on. At the same time I am trying to clean up piles of poop on the floor, my cake is burning, I was late to take Donny to his tutoring class, and he and Laura and Jay are walking around with cloths in front of their faces because of the smell. Then Mom decided to throw a tantrum, and I had to keep running back and forth sitting her down and picking up those darn piles of poop on the floor. Then we had to go to the doctor's. He kept saying to Mom, "Take a deep breath," and she would whisper, "I don't know how to do that." He would show her, and she would forget in the next minute. I tried to help, and she told me to "Shut up, don't show me, do it yourself." She refused to get out of the van afterward, kept smacking my hands. She wore her gloves during dinner, and Dad was saying, "Do you have mates for these socks?"

January 30, 2000

I ran over the garbage can yesterday with the van. I got it so lodged that I had to call AAA to come and dislodge it. While they were on their way, I had a tantrum and was throwing garbage into the street, jumping up and down on the can to see if I could dislodge it and/or revving the engine to see if it would just shoot away. AAA took care of it. And then I just sat and laughed. Humor most definitely helps! All this caretaking comes down to love and loving and showing love. I am trying to embrace all of these sufferings. Mostly I am not doing very well.

Tonight Dad talked about how we have to keep her from getting upset about going to a home. I wasn't aware that we were that far in that direction, but it must have been on his mind. Lord help him, he is afraid. Whenever you think that I am doing a good job, re-read this one or others that speak of how imperfect I am. It is a very long road to goodness, obedience and love, at least the kind He talks about. Pray for me.

February 2, 2000

Dad seems to have no depth perception anymore. When Mom is off to the side, he can't see her. Only when he looks straight on is he able to see her. The doctor suggested he come and be checked out. We finally have a Home Health nurse who comes a couple of days a week.

The doctor said he thinks Dad is depressed. I so agree with him. He said it in front of Dad which was good. He will get a pill like Mom has to see if that helps. Dad is trying so hard to keep it all together, and he can't do it anymore. He said to the doctor, "This is too hard on me." I am glad that he said it out loud. Mom, on the other hand, when she knows that she has gotten out of hand, always comes back and tries to say something that says how much she appreciates him and his goodness. She, too, is trying to hold it together. And me? Well, I sure hope that when and if that time comes that Mom has to go into a nursing home, that someone will go with me because the thought fills me with a lot of pain.

February 10, 2000

Mom is into doesn't-want-this, doesn't-want-that, doesn't-want-the other. It must be very hard for her with everyone telling her what to do, what to eat, what to wear, and she is tired.

February 12, 2000

George, Dad is just not together. Yesterday, he went to bed at 2:30 in the afternoon, teeth out and everything. He got up at 6:00 p.m. and thought it was morning. I was feeding them dinner, and he said, "Mom keeps thinking this is my supper." I said, "It is, Dad." He said, "Well, what time is it, what day is it, isn't George coming tomorrow?" Later on after getting Mom ready for bed, I came upstairs and asked Dad if he was going to bed again. He did.

This morning at 6:00 he calls me from the hallway, "Linda, what time is it?" I said, "6:00, Dad." He said, "George comes today? Is Don going to work? Is it time to eat dinner?" "No, Dad, it's breakfast time." I think I am going to cut the anti-depressant in half. I like it that he is smiling more these days. They probably will be fine when you are here, George, and you will think it is I who needs a home, but not a nursing one. Love me.

February 26, 2000

It was a wonderful time with George being here. A respite for sure. Each of us brings something to this caretaking thing. I guess mine is poop clean up, just kidding, but George read to them, that was nice, and Susan is such a "take care of" person. Dad really counts on her to help him with his "shoebox business affairs."

Mom is really "hot" these days. She walks around like a caged lion, up and down and up and down, several times an hour. Today she was up early taking her clothes off and walking around the bed. She actually is interested again in doing things but doesn't know how to do them. She put clothes on the vacuum cleaner, hid my purse in the garbage bag, kept insisting that I do the clothes right now and wasn't taking "no" for an answer. I kept saying, "Mom, I'll do it when I'm ready." She didn't like that. She was on Laura constantly, and one time told her she couldn't drink in the living room. Jay said that Mom told Laura she had to drink it in some room that he had never heard of. When Laura ignored her, she went over to her and repeated it louder. I remember Mom doing that to me when I was young. So, it has deteriorated around here with Laura, poor little one. I don't even care if she ignores Mom right now when she does those things, Mom is harsh and unbending. It is a constant question of what to do with meds, give more, less, half? What do you guys think? Today she was a pistol! Talk later.

March 3, 2000

This morning Mom and Dad minced around each other at the doorway while I am trying to come downstairs with their breakfast. We did a dance for awhile until finally Dad opened the door and got out of the way. They ate, Dad came upstairs and said that Mom was giving him fits because she kept putting the Kleenex in the bowl, and then he would take it out, and she would put it back in. Why, might one ask, did he bother to take it out? Anyway, that question unanswered, I will continue. Then Mom went to bed with only her under things on, and she draped a jacket over her neck. Hmm. Dad came upstairs to ask if I would watch her while he fussed with the garbage. I would call what he was wanting to do pucker butting, but I said, "Sure." Every once in a while Mom would peek up and look at the garage door and say, "Linda?" "Yes, Mom?" "There is an animal out there." "No, it's just Dad." Five minutes later, "Linda?" "Yes, Mom?" "I think the animal is scratching at the door." "Mom, it's just Dad with the garbage." Five or ten minutes later, up her head came. "Well, I am throwing up." I gulped and said, "What?" She said, "I am trying to grow up." There was no logic downstairs today.

March 6, 2000

Mom is having trouble with being backed up. She doesn't drink water, doesn't like water, therefore, she is having trouble. She has pain in her back, pain in her stomach. I realized that she hadn't gone to the bathroom for about five days. It is amazing how much stuff I have to keep in my head with my parents' issues. The health aide came over, and as we talked, we decided to give her a suppository. It took a while to convince Mom of what a good idea this was. Dad was standing around with visits to the bathroom every 15 minutes or so. He was probably visualizing that he was getting this done to himself. The suppository didn't work. I finally took her to the doctor after an hour or so, and after much prodding and poking, she was given a shot to relax her and let her rest. By the time we got home she was amazingly loopy, or shall I say, loopier than normal. The nurse told me that she would probably sleep and be out of it. However, she failed to tell me that Mom would probably shuffle in place for awhile before she actually went anywhere. Dad, thinking she was moving, shuffled in place with her. I am standing there trying not to laugh but not succeeding at all. Finally, Dad figured out that they were not moving, and he started to laugh. We finally got her to where she needed to be, and then it was night. I hope none of you think I am being disrespectful, they are funny. I told them that they reminded me of Abbott and Costello. They thought that was funny too. I have to laugh, or I will cry.

March 9, 2000 - The "she" is me.

It was very early in the morning, and she knew she had to use the bathroom. It was cold, and she was tired and didn't want to get up but reasoned that if she didn't, she wouldn't be able to go back to sleep. Oh, well, have to do it. She had just fallen asleep again when suddenly she woke with her husband saying, "Hello," quite loudly. Her father opened the door and said, "Hello." She quickly looked at the clock. It said in bright red numbers 2:16. She looked at her father's form silhouetted in the half light from the hall and asked, "Does Mom need to go to the bathroom?" He replied, "No, I am just trying to get her up." "Dad, it's only 2:00 in the morning." She knew she had to get up. She could tell that he wasn't getting that. Resentment rising, she quickly thought of how sad it is to see fear in his face when he does something stupid, fear of her reactions. So, she swallowed the resentment, resolving to be as cheerful as possible.

She followed him down the hall where her mother was lying on the bed moaning saying she had to get up. "I will help you up, Mom." "Nooo, I can't," she says. "Okay, Mom, can you turn on your side, it might be easier?" "No, no, I can't." As she stands there listening to the dialogue, she reckons that somewhere in the place that memories are stored, she was once small, and her mother must have stood by her while she

31

said, "No, no, I can't do it," whatever it was she couldn't do, and whether patiently or impatiently, her mother stood there and waited, and here she was doing the same thing now for her mother. Her father meanwhile was talking about how he thought it was morning, and that he went upstairs and saw a man with a gray robe on walking through the house. He went everywhere but the recording studio, and he just needed to figure out who the gray robed man was. Just in case you don't know this, Jay has a makeshift recording studio in the laundry room.

It was too early for her to try to make sense of it, so she just listened and hoped it would relax him. It is too wearying to take care of them right now, too many health problems with her Mom, and then again she thought, to travel down that road was futile and destructive for her own attitude. She offered up a prayer, HELP, and hoped that God would answer and help.

Her husband got up while she was making tea for them, and they laughed and rolled their eyes. He, fortunately, was able to go back to sleep. Not she, the die had been cast. So, with a sigh she got up. She was trying to be very quiet, even though her parents were up watching television. She is wanting to keep a small portion of the day for herself, prayers have been uttered, she is watching the storm rage outside, snow and heavy winds that bend the trees and blow the snow in a straight line. It is like the wildness she feels inside of her, the storms of conflicting emotions that rise up and then die down as God calms the wind and the waves. It would be such peace to live each moment to the fullest, to live each moment as best she could knowing that she will never have that moment to redo, but it is such a hard thing to do. One moment, two, she can do, but moments upon moments stretching out as far as the day allows bring a small voice inside of her crying out, no, no, I can't do it. And just as she coaxed her Mom, yes, Mom you can, you already have, I will help you, we will do it a little at a time, she can hear the Lord say, yes, you can, you already have, I will help you, we will do it...

March 10, 2000 - Some chapter.

I found my compassion failing last night. We were in the ER, again. I had tried to get Mom to drink some water so that she could take a pill that would help her. Mom refused again. We did the same routine, "It hurts, Linda." "I know, Mom, will you take this pill?" "No, I don't want it, it hurts." I finally said, "We should go to the ER, would you go?" She said she would. In her before Alzheimer's state she wouldn't have gone, but then in her before Alzheimer's state she wouldn't be having this problem, but back to my opening statement.

As I sat in the ER watching my Mom while she lay in the bed, there was mercy somewhere inside of me. I watched and realized that she wasn't worried about who was there with her, this was different. Usually she would have been calling out for Nor, but she wasn't. She just kept looking at her hands and arms. Suddenly a migraine intruded itself on my brain, and I sat feeling more and more like a patient.

Dad and I changed places every once in a while. At one point he reached out his hand and said, "Let's pray," and though I held on to his hand, my mind couldn't comprehend praying. I was too tired, too sore, too self consumed with the enormity of it all. The doctor asked what I wanted them to do, and I said, "I want you to keep her overnight and help her. Her needs are far too much for me to handle, and I don't know what to do." This wonderful, kind doctor heard me, she understood. Prayer is answered even when I am not in it, even when I don't feel like praying. But back to my opening statement.

We waited long, long hours for a bed in the hospital. We changed places, Dad and Don and I, walking around each other, pacing like three lions who have no idea where to go or what to do, not speaking or very little. Mom does her mumbling talk, cries. I was powerless. My head hurt, my heart hurt, her tears hurt, but I could not help. I felt drained. I walked through the ER halls so strangely that one of the nurses watched me for awhile. I felt like I was drugged, like a person walking through thick oil slowly turning my head.

This morning as I walked to Mom's room, I found that place inside again, compassion I mean. I am so glad it wasn't completely gone. It was just empty and needed refilling. If it was left for me to fill up, it would be abysmally empty and insincere, only God can do that. I breathe another sigh of relief, and even though my head still hurts, I can look at Mom again with my heart.

We have made a decision with the social worker from the hospital that Mom will be placed in a nursing home. I know that I can no longer run this way. Mom's needs far surpass anything I can do, and she is not safe at home. Right before she was having this current trouble, she was found in someone else's house wandering around. When Dad was asked about all of this, he spoke about the garbage and how he had gotten the papers out to be picked up. He cannot or doesn't want to make the decision to do this. I understand. Along with my husband Don, Susan and George we have made it for him. I understand, 60 years is a very long time, even when you are failing yourself. Somehow that marriage contract never quits. I understand. With love.

March 18, 2000 - Beginning tales from the third floor.

What and how do I start? Susan and I have observed these days together, and it is much easier to do with two. Dad is lost without his partner and lost without his reason to exist, and now he has to find somewhere inside of him a reason to continue living instead of just care giving. At 85 it would seem not an easy thing to do. Mom is in a nursing home, a very good one, it comes with many recommendations, and certainly from our observations everyone is friendly, and they try at all costs to do everything possible to make their patients comfortable and happy, at least as happy as one can be there.

Mom spent the first two days quite adjusted, and then last night and today was very combative and angry at the world and refusing to do much of anything. Susan and I rescued her for a little while by coming and talking to her, but we weren't getting anywhere. Her anger included us, no offense taken.

Perhaps I can describe the third floor to you. When you get off the elevator you are immediately in the middle of the hallway. To the right or the left the hallway stretches on either side, and one end has two chairs with a table in the middle, and at the other end there is a small couch. Windows are at each end. The rooms are on both sides of this hallway. Close to the elevators is the nursing station or an alcove where the nurse's office is. And right across from that on the other side of the hall is the dayroom, a large room where everyone can congregate for whatever. That's pretty much it.

Watching everyone in this circle of women is an interesting thing in itself. One we have named Racer. She is in an odd walker and walks from one end and around to the other. She comes right up to you, chews her gums a bit, adjusts her glasses, stares at you and speeds off. She never stops, she never runs into anyone, no small feat believe me, and she just keeps running.

Then there is the lady that one of the other women call the All Day Sucker, aptly named. She licks and licks her lips and nose around and around. I can't imagine how chapped her lips must be. She bangs on everything she comes near, and she yells when she bangs.

There is a lady who we have named Chirper. She is in a wheelchair and chirps like a bird most of the time. She doesn't talk, just chirps.

Another woman, whom we named the Singer, has a lovely voice and can sing lots of songs, but today she was cold and was walking around and singing in a sing-song voice, "He-at-er, la la la, can't someone turn on the he-at-er." Susan commented that it was like a movie we had seen, and suddenly she and I got the giggles and couldn't stop. Tears were running down our cheeks, and I kept snorting, we just couldn't help it. Even Mom started smiling and giggling. Finally, Dad got frustrated with us, and although Susan was the instigator, once again, I was the one who got yelled at. Some things never change. But we still found it hard to stop laughing.

Mom thinks everyone on the floor is all nuts and can't understand why she is there. She looks as if she feels that we have abandoned her, I am not offended. There are times when I feel as if I did something wrong or perhaps didn't do enough, and then I remember the times in these last few months, and I know that no matter how much I would like to continue in my heart, I cannot, nor can my Dad, nor can my family. It is heartbreaking, however, for all of us.

She has a very nice roommate who seems to be about the same as Mom. How can one really tell though? They all seem okay until they come out with something that makes you know where they are. I look at them and wonder what they were like before this disease. Mom I know, but what about them?

And so that is the best I can say for today. I am relearning how to sleep, I will miss Susan when she goes, I miss Mom, I don't know how to reach Dad. So, until the next time. Love, me.

March 24, 2000

Mom ate last night, at least about 25 percent of the meal, and drank several glasses of water and ate sherbet. This is a major feat considering the last few days there has been little to no drinking and/or eating.

Mom was having a horrible time, and, of course, that translates into Dad and I having a horrible time. Each day Dad and I would go there and find her in a fetal position in bed, so small and thin that it looks as if she isn't even there except for her little head of white, gray hair. No movement, no response to us except an occasional grunt when asked a question, and she was pretty choosy about which questions she would grunt at. No response to Dad, which is very hard for him. No I love you, no I am so tired, or my back hurts, nothing. I have asked the nurses, I have asked other people, I have done some reading on placement in homes, and pretty much they all say that it is an adjustment.

However, knowing Mom, I think it is more. I can see the look on her face, a betrayed look, a punishing look. I have tried everything in my bag of tricks, that translates into what I did as a child to win some favor or such, but nothing works. When my children were little and were throwing a tantrum or trying to punish me (which seems to be the consensus of opinion from the experts there that Mom is throwing a tantrum) I could at least love them into some sort of truce for a minute or tease them into it, and with them there would be some sort of response, but not with Mom, and it is hard.

Each day I hope for a change, and each day I dread going up to the third floor, not knowing what will await. And unfortunately, her room is easily seen from the elevator. You cannot imagine the hope I have and how quickly it is dashed. Even understanding how Mom must feel and not blaming her for being angry, still I hope for some logic in her mind and understanding that I could not do anything different. I find that little girl in me still reacting to Mom's rejection and anger and hope that God heals that place in me so that I can just love her without judging. I am so sorry for her and Dad, but I always keep in the back of my mind that God in His vast and perfect knowledge knows just what we need and when. I bow to that once more.

One day one of the nurses who has been there a very long time said, "Did you tell her the truth about her being here?" Oops. No, we didn't. For so long Mom had never wanted to go to a nursing home, and even though she had told Dad that if she got really bad to take her to a home, we had not told her that this was the time she was staying, so we kept saying that it was only for a little while. A lie, and once one lies, it is hard to back pedal and make things right.

Today I went up there, she was lying in the bed as usual, eyes closed, she wasn't asleep, and I knelt down by the bed facing her and said, "Mom, I just wanted to tell you why you are here in this nursing home. You are here because your needs are more than I can handle. You are unsafe in the house, and Dad doesn't know how to help you anymore." She said, "So what," ah, that was something. " I know, Mom, you don't want to be here, but if you remember with Grandma Koetke you could no longer take care of her, and you had to put her in a nursing home." She said, "M-hm." So, I reminded her that Dad and I would come each day, and that I hoped she wouldn't be angry with us anymore. "I am sorry," I told her, "and I love you." She said, "I love you too."

March 25, 2000

Each day when we get off the elevator, Arlene (Mom's roommate), greets us with a smile and hello. She is obviously adjusted, and it is such a pleasure. She greets us with, "I hope everyone is hungry," and you just know that when she was younger and in charge of a family, she said that same thing, "I hope everyone is hungry."

Yesterday I got off the elevator and noticed a lady in a wheelchair with her brows knit furiously together and her hand on her face as if she were in pain and a scowl on her mouth. She sat against the wall as close to the wall as she could get without becoming a part of the plaster. She snapped at anyone who even touched her chair. She was so angry, tears were so close to her eyes, you could tell that even at a glance. She was frightened and confused and mad as hell. She had only been there a couple of days, and she is going through the same thing as our Mom. No matter how loving the nurses and aides are, and believe me they are, it must be like being thrown into a foreign land with no one you can talk to and no one who understands you, and you have nowhere you can call home, and dangers lurk everywhere, even if they really don't. In a way it was helpful for me to see this lady, though I feel for her, because it meant that Mom isn't the only one, she isn't picking me just to pick on. She will come through this, and it will pass, as all things do. So, we take joy in each meal eaten, in each drink of water that makes it down her throat, and in simple things, such as getting her hair washed or getting a manicure.

March 26, 2000

Dad lived yesterday. I know it may sound strange, but he did. He went to the home as always and just sat there as always. When he came home, he spent an hour talking to a man down the street. We ate dinner, went to Laura's concert at school, went to Dairy Queen and enjoyed a sundae, came home, he talked to a friend on the phone, watched a little basketball and went to bed at a respectable 10 p.m. and slept soundly. I was so glad that he felt life outside of the nursing home. He even told one lady sitting next to him at the concert that he had been married for 60 years, and then the tears brimmed in his eyes. Even that is good in my book. I was thankful for last night. Today is another day, and we hope.

April 1, 2000

Mom has been adjusting pretty well lately. Her skin tears are healing, and there haven't been any falls for a while. She is beginning to wave at some of the other ladies, which obviously means that she is beginning to recognize them. Dad enjoys observing all the doings and goings on and reports them to me, funny and sad, when he can remember them.

Today when I went there, Racer made a beeline over to me. All Day Sucker, who had been in bed for a few days, is now up more and moving around in her wheelchair again, a good thing to see. She met me in the hall today and tried to stop me by yelling at me. I smiled and continued on. There is a tiny lady who cries a lot whenever she sees someone or whenever she feels like it, she seems very much lost. She always wears a pointy hat on her head and walks up and down with her little white hair and hat and one sock on and one sock off. She sounds like a nursery rhyme. Then there is another lady who is always angry and hits me when I'm in her presence. She says, "What are ya doing, don't do that!" I tried to help her the other day with her exercises, and she responded for a minute, then got angry again. I hope she finds some peace, and, yep, she is nicknamed The Angry One.

We all know who they are by their nicknames, even the kids do, and they haven't even seen them yet. They are a little leery about seeing them, they don't relish seeing all the yucky stuff, their word, not mine. They have gone there but just haven't stayed very long.

Mom is eating well, and they have finally handled her pain, a continuous muscle relaxant, and she seems to feel better. Tonight she wanted to talk to Dad, so the nurse dialed the phone, and as soon as Dad answered the phone, she put the phone down and walked away. This seems to happen whenever she calls, perhaps she just wants to hear his voice or else forgets why she is holding the phone.

April 6, 2000

The love seat was situated underneath the window of the nurse's station. It's an inviting place to sit. The little alcove is bathed in muted light. A place where little groups of ladies gather, a place where lots of things happen, snacks and medicines get passed out there, the nurses are there talking and busy about their duties. This particular evening the couch was inhabited by three ladies, Caroline (Singer), Mabel (Racer), and Laura Mae (Mom). All three are holding hands and swinging their legs enjoying watching what was going on around them. I could imagine that this is how Mom sat with her two friends Teeny and Annabelle many years ago. But to Mom, many years ago doesn't have the same significance as it once did. In front of these three sat another friend, Arlene, who was busy feeding them ice cream from the same spoon and dish.

The three, and now the feeder, were having such a grand time. Pretty soon the nurse came to get Mom, and as she left Mabel said, "Take care of her, she's mine." The nurse said she wished she had a camera, the picture was worth a thousand smiles. It is what we all hoped would take place, some bonding, a connection, a friend or two to help these hours pass by less lonely. It is quite a thing to watch. We start out with innocence, uninhibited as children, and sometimes we end up again as children, uninhibited, just enjoying a friendship, not caring how it looks to someone else. It seems that touch is very important on this floor. It might be a brief moment and may not return for a while, but the joy it brings to those of us who watch and hope is of great value.

First of all, just the fact that Mom was eating out of the same dish and spoon of another person, let alone three others, is mind boggling, I do so wish there had been a camera. I don't yet know the other two ladies well, but Arlene, the feeder, is the same lady who is hoping that everyone is hungry and good and happy.

She, Mom, and Dad were in the room today having a rather lopsided conversation, one in which you are never sure where one conversation ends and another begins. It is an art to try to understand how their minds work, but I think Arlene is rubbing off on Mom. I asked Arlene how she was, and, of course, she was good today. When I asked Mom, instead of her usual answer, "Oh, I guess okay," she said, "I am good." Can I stand two goods, yep!! And Mom is eating all of her food, like Arlene, and now we know that she is even eating Arlene's ice cream. In case you couldn't tell, a good day, a sigh of relief day. When the Lord says, "Don't worry," I will try to think of this day and know that each day has enough troubles and joys of its own.

April 8, 2000

Arlene came into her room, and as we were sitting on the bed, I said, "Hello, Arlene," and for the next several minutes this good and happy and hungry lady was very confused. She wanted to know how I knew her, where her bed was, does she sleep here, who sleeps in the room with her, when and where would she eat? She says she has never eaten in the dining room, and now if she could lie down on that bed for just a few moments, would someone tell her when she can eat? She didn't know how she got here or where she was, and she thinks she is going crazy, at which point Mom looked at me and rolled her eyes. I helped Arlene as best I could while her bell kept going off when she would try to stand up, and then I finally went and got help so she could get in her bed.

Helen, no nickname yet, and Mabel (Racer) collided the other day, and I saw a nurse come over, disengage them, and then comforted both of them. It was very encouraging to me. I can leave Mom there without worrying about someone being mean to her. But no matter how good a place it is, I am learning that I need to be as proactive and present as I can. I had no idea about that before.

Racer is really something. I look at her face and want to comfort her. She has a scared little girl's face. There are times when I wonder what wounds lie hidden in her mind. If I ever questioned the truth of everyone having a little child inside, I will remember seeing the little children in each one of these dear ladies on the third floor

I hope on my visit tomorrow to have more things to report, more stories to share. I hope you don't mind these introductions to our new friends. They are a part of Mom's life right now, and I guess in a way ours. They visit when they want, and sometimes Dad has to shush Helen and say, "Our Mom is sleeping," and Helen just looks, takes a blanket from the room, and walks out. At first when we would go there, Susan and I would just giggle and be nervous, but as we have gotten to know the ladies, the nervousness has passed, and now we just shake our heads and smile. The disease is awful, but "they" are not, and they make me smile. They still have personalities, I don't know what I expected, but they are still their own persons.

April 18, 2000

The floor was very quiet, different from the daytime. It wasn't really that late, but getting off the elevator the mood of the place was less busy and almost eerie. There were several knots of women sitting close to the tables, a stray one now and then sitting apart. I looked at the faces in the dining room and didn't see Mom. I looked in her room, still no sign of her. Then I saw her slowly walking down the hall looking into each room, waving sometimes, and other times just looking, and then on to the next room. She is so little and frail, except you know when she holds your hand how very strong she is. Over her shirt she had on a vest that she had tried to put on, but got so confused that she just left it hanging over one shoulder, and the other shoulder was bare. No one really thinks twice about that kind of strange dressing here. We might not imagine stepping out of the house dressed strangely (well, I might), but here on this floor pretty much most anything goes. Mom had tried to dress herself, that is the important thing, she tried, some sense of independence that says I am still me. We visited, she ate, still trying to be social, as she kept offering me food.

Then we walked a bit, finally sitting down when she said how tired she was and how hard it is to go to sleep unless someone holds her. My breath caught, and there was a lump in my throat, a sob in my heart, and I patted her head on my shoulder. She allowed me to help her get ready for bed, comb her hair and cover her up, but I heard that as soon as I had gone she was back up. She walks all night till midnight, she and many others, looking for something, someone. In Mom's case, someone to hold her till she falls asleep.

As we were eating dinner Caroline (Singer) started singing a real song and enjoyed the attention. Then Mabel (Racer) was talking so rationally and intelligently without all the tears that I couldn't imagine it was the same little lady who runs up and down the halls. Mom would smile as she went by them and often tells the nurses that she will take care of the patients because, after all, she was a nurse. They don't mind, they let her help. Mom calls almost every night looking for us to pick her up. That is the hardest. Sometimes she gets angry, but most of the time when we say we will come tomorrow, she is then all right.

Tonight the nurse told me that every night at 8:00 p.m. they put a movie on, and when it is the Little Rascals, Mom must have Little Rascals radar because she makes a beeline for the television and sits and watches. Susan and I laugh at that because it is so not like Mom to even watch television. Dad goes every day and sits while she sleeps, perhaps it is the one time when she feels safe and can sleep while he is there. I believe it makes him feel useful and gives him a sense that he is still taking care of her. When I relay some of this to Susan, she and I will at times ooh and aah, much as you would do for a baby or child when they did something that catches your heartstrings, and that is how they are, like children, and often they are so cute, as old as they are. They are so vulnerable, and that is part of what makes them so cute, perhaps strange sounding, but true. It is a new lesson every day. Love, me.

April 25, 2000

Easter was wonderful, and we had a nice visit with Mom when she came home. She was tired when we took her back, but we all had a nice time. One of the nurses told me that one day Mom danced an entire dance with her. In fact, I heard Mom say on the phone, "We danced good." I know that the third floor is a much more stimulating place for Mom than here at home.

I learned that Mabel (Racer) is 89 years old. As Donny said, "She has something to cry about." Arlene (Happy and Hungry) wanted Dad to help her with her "bathrooming" the other day, and as soon as she started speaking about that, he walked out of the room. You know I cracked up. He sees all kinds of things. Dad is adjusting as well as he can too. He is very confused, especially at night. I think it is just stress. The last two nights he has done well, and I hope this trend continues. The peace of Christ be with you as well as with me.

April 30, 2000

Everyday Mom gets a visit from Dad and most of the time from me. She seems to be comfortable with knowing that someone will visit. Today Donny and I went to visit and pick up Dad. He was looking pretty bleak. He had decided for some unknown reason to not eat lunch, they feed him along with Mom, and so he was very hungry. He may have been trying to avoid some kind of problem with Mom. She gave him a hard time yesterday, inappropriate behavior, which does happen at times, and he wasn't prepared for it. Mom was quite cheerful today as we sat at the end of the hall looking at the ladies who congregate in the middle by the nurse's station and the individuals who break away from the pack to walk the halls and look in the rooms.

Today we saw Racer. We haven't seen her in a while. She raced down to us and got real close and then turned, and off she sped. Mom asked, "Why do all the women chew on something here?" She makes faces when they aren't looking. I know she doesn't mean to be mean, and it doesn't come off like that, she is being like a five year old who is just mimicking what she sees.

Then along came Helen, whom we have named Picker, because she is always picking at her clothes or someone else's. Halfway down the hall she ducked into a room and kept peeking out of the room at us. Then slowly she came out and started again towards us. She pushed a lady in her wheelchair for a while (I am not sure the lady in the wheelchair wanted to be pushed), and finally, there she was right there with us, twisting her shirt like a little one who didn't know quite what was expected of her. She, too, was making chewing gestures, and Mom stared at her and said to Donny, "You won't get to interview her, you know." I saw at one point for one whole moment in time, Mom and Helen stare at each other, they locked eyes. I cannot imagine what passed between them, some kind of understanding it seemed, then it passed, they disengaged, and Helen walked away. It looked as if she wanted to converse but has no clue how to start or what to say.

Pretty soon Rosie (Two Timer) came sauntering down the hall. She is a 50-ish woman who exercises with her arms as she walks. Mom said, "You won't get anything from her." Rosie spoke a few sentences, I notice she repeats certain words. "I will will go away, so you can can have have a happy happy time," it is a strange language, and off she went quite amiably. I could see Singer and All Day Sucker and Chirper and even Racer walking (and speeding) around looking quite confused, but none of the rest ventured down our way. Even Happy and Hungry was there. I think they were waiting for dinner, certainly Happy and Hungry was.

There are a couple of new ladies on the floor. I don't see them too much, my visits have not been as long lately. As I watch these ladies I think of my Mom's life. She is a wife, a daughter, a mom, a nurse, a missionary, and so much more. She had likes and dislikes, she got angry (well, she still gets angry). She loved the ocean and walking in the waves. She loved Wauhob Lake and sunbathing and picking wildflowers. She loved to cook and bake and didn't like housework much. She had and still has at times a wonderful sense of humor and enjoyed laughing at silly things. Even though so many of those things are lost, they are still a part of the totality of her.

I wonder as I look at the other ladies what wonderful depths and mysteries are locked up. Perhaps I will know more when I next write. Until then, love you.

May 2, 2000

This afternoon I had a chance to sit a while with Mom. As we were in her room talking, Happy and Hungry came in and started talking about one thing and another, and pretty soon they were waving to each other, and Mom was finishing Happy and Hungry's sentences, and believe me I had no idea what they were talking about. Then Singer walked by, looked in, and stopped. Immediately Mom said, "Come and sit with me in the chair." You could tell that there was a friendship there. How long it would last is anyone's guess. They seem to be very mischievous, you can almost see it in their eyes. I would have enjoyed watching them a bit longer, but I had to leave, and Singer said she had to go and check all the other beds.

When I came by tonight, the nurse said that Mom and Singer walk up and down the halls holding hands and getting into things. I knew it. One night they were having a sleep over. They were trading nightgowns and going to sleep in this little bed. Mom is tiny, but Singer not so much, so the nurse had to separate them. Any and every story is something to share. They follow each other around no matter where they go apparently. The nurses enjoy having a good time with them. I'm glad because I know that connecting with someone else is the best thing that can happen with Mom. In some ways I feel sad that I don't get to see all the funny and poignant things Mom does, kind of like when the kids went off to school for the first time.

Dad doesn't know what to make of it all. I know that he feels sad that Mom doesn't only need him all the time. In his heart though I know he knows this is a good thing.

I did find out that Singer has two children, girls. She thinks that they are still in high school, and that her husband got "months" (mumps) from them. Mom thought that "months" was a funny disease to get, and sadly enough, Dad thought that Singer knew what she was talking about. Mom seems to be having fun, for that I am thankful. Love, me

May 7, 2000

Well, today Mom had sweatpants, a skirt and nightgown on all together and would not take any of it off. She was very insistent that she liked her outfit. She has so little control over her life that when she does get stubborn, it makes me smile. It was a good visit today. I notice Mom is a bit more feisty of late, and I never really know when that will come out. She is very tender with Racer and Picker. She holds Picker's hand and says, "She won't talk to you." I heard Racer talk today, not cry, but talk, and she was very lucid. She is actually sometimes quite clear. Today she shook her head, smiled and said, "I'm tired," and then kept on walking. That may not sound like a big deal, but it is.

There is a new lady on the floor, I call her Leather Gloves. She always has on these thick, black leather gloves. No matter what she has on or how hot it is, she wears those gloves. Her real name is Shirley. Today as Mom and I walked the halls, we happened to walk by the nurse's station where Leather Gloves and Singer were sitting on the couch. I stopped and spoke to them, and Leather Gloves says, "Do I know you?" I said, "No, but I am Laura Mae's daughter." Apparently these three hang out together a lot. So, she gushed, "Oh, come over here and meet me." So, of course, I did, and as she took my hand (I am convinced that people with Alzheimer's are extra strong) the conversation went like this:

Leather Gloves: "How nice it is to meet you."

Me: "Yes, I'm glad that I am meeting you."

As Singer grabs my hand, she whispered.

Singer: "Can you help us to escape?"

Me: "Well, Caroline, I think you are quite safe here."

Singer: "Oh, no, I am afraid for my life."

Me: "I will watch out for you."

She seemed quite satisfied with that, but shortly after I overheard her whispering to the nurse that she might be ready for a nursing home.

Oh, dear, they do crack me up. They are all precious. They have this little city on that floor, and they go up and down, and each one has their own characteristics and obviously their own little schticks. Mom is quite feisty when we are not around, so they are thinking of changing her room to Singer's since Mom is in her room most of the time. The other night the nurse said that Mom and Singer were fussing around the nurse's cart, and pretty soon they brought her a diaper, holding it out like it was some kind of holy thing and said that "Arequcksquatchiacomo" (that's what it sounded like she said) "needed this diaper," and it was all the nurse could do to keep from laughing. They were very serious, and the more the nurse questioned them, the more they got the giggles. I did see Happy and Hungry today, she is the same, still making sure she gets dinner. I saw Picker, she sometimes almost talks to me. I saw Racer, who really looks like she is in her 60s, and Chirper was busy chirping from around the corner. Can you just see it? Love you all.

May 20, 2000 - I have a group name for you, updaters.

At the end of the hall there is a loveseat. I always know that I will see Mom and Singer and Leather Gloves seated on the loveseat in varying stages of sleep. It is right in front of the office window, and Mom likes to sit there where she can see everything. So often when I am dealing with Mom I think of my kids when they were little. It is really like taking care of a child.

Today Singer was with her on the love seat, Dad was standing, and I could tell he was getting ready to go home. Mom was happy to see me, said my name, introducing me to her friend for the umpteenth time and then told her how she had Susan, George and the other one. We have yet to figure out who the other one is. As we all sat looking at one another, Singer said to Mom, "Let's go home." Mom said, "Oh, no, we don't want to do that," as she grabbed Singer's hand. Singer said, "Well, I have to clean the church, so I guess I'll stay." Their conversation continued on about how sometimes she comes here, and it is such a "pig place," and she doesn't understand how it can get like that and how she really likes a clean church. When questioned about where she lives, she said, "Far away." Mom the whole time was nodding in agreement at all her friend was saying. Pretty soon down the hall came a lady called June, who I named The Boss. She seems like an angry lady who must have been in charge of a lodge somewhere when she was younger. She said loudly, "Well, are you going to lock up and are you all right?" I responded, "Yes, we were all right, and yes, I would lock up," which launched a whole thing on how many doors did I have, and did I have it all sorted out which ones I would lock, and where were the keys, and would I go get them, and that she would like to help. That started

Singer out, and then both of them were talking at once, and neither seemed perturbed at that at all. They just talked until they were done. Suddenly it was quiet and Mom said, "Now, you are into it, and you can't get out of it," and she was right. The Boss was not content with my agreeable answers. She looked at Dad standing there and said, "You aren't taking care of him very well, and he deserves more respect than that." I again answered agreeably and told her that I would do better, which launched her into another version of what keys she needed. Finally, she drifted off, and Singer said, "That lady can't help clean the church, she's too old." That wasn't the end. Mom informed the aide that she couldn't have Norm, and then we all laughed except Dad who did his Jack Benny impersonation. Even Singer thought it was funny. It was time for Dad and I to go, and Mom was content to stay where she was and waved goodbye. As we were waiting for the elevator, I looked back and saw Mom with one foot on the couch, her arms around that leg, and she and Singer were deep into some conversation that only they knew what they were talking about. Some days they don't even acknowledge each other but today was a sweet connection. Sigh......

May 24, 2000 - The "she" is me, again.

She ran up the back stairs expecting to see them sitting on the couch at the end of the hall. Instead, there was her Dad by himself. She could see her Mom trying to push a large cart while an aide standing four feet away was asking her Mom if she wanted some juice. It looked every bit like a standoff scene from Gunsmoke, and somehow she was Festus, the comic relief, who just happened innocently upon the scene and was trying to guffaw his way into the fray. It was quiet for a minute, but then rippling down the hall could be heard, "The daughter is here" each time getting softer until it died out at the nurse's station. Once more, she had no idea how to proceed with yet another new situation with her Mom. Tentatively, she approached her mother from behind but speaking softly said, "Hi, Mom, what ya doin?" As her mother turned, she could see the set lines around her mouth, her teeth were tightly clamped together, determined in whatever she was trying to do. She asked her, "What are you pushing the cart for?" The mumbled response was something about the kids not knowing what they were doing. Well, of course, what else? Shrugging, she just started to push the cart with her mother, asking questions as they walked, trying to find a way to dissuade her cart pushing. As they neared the nurse's station, it was like some wagon train from the east that had finally crossed the western border. The nurse approached, but stayed out of reach, and said softly, "Your Mom was hitting another client, and we had to disengage her. She scratched an aide's face, and when your father stopped her, she bit his arm. Do you think you might be able to get her to take her medicine?" She felt so bad for her father. That bite must have hurt his heart more than his arm, so she said, "I'll try," but was leery herself. She wasn't looking to upset her Mom more than she already was.

All of this conversation lasted only a moment or two, and though her mother listened for a minute, she continued her journey down the long hall. She had to run counter interference with some of the wheelchair bound patients. Once they ran into another cart and a piece of heavy machinery. At last, she thought, this would deter her mother, but her mother just kept saying, "What's wrong with this darn thing?" and tried to keep going. While she was trying to help steer the cart away from the blockage, she noticed her Mom's finger with a painful looking cramp in it. It didn't seem to make any difference. She could see her Mom wince, but in spite of it, she pressed on. Finally, they arrived at the other end of the hall. She went to get the medicine disguised in ice cream, brought it back and fed it to her mother while she was "taking a break." They sat for a few minutes talking, her Mom taking a sip of tea, then pouring it on her feet and the floor and just as quickly as that the break was over, and they pushed the cart all the way to the other end where her father still sat, nursing his wounded arm and heart.

At that place of gathering, Racer got in the way, so she had to stand in front of the cart trying in vain to move Racer out of the way saying, "I think someone is looking for you," and Racer responding by moving on. An aide took over so she could take her father home. During the journey down the "hall country," she asked her mother if she could have a hug. "Of course," was the reply, but the hug was stiff and detached. It was a gift nonetheless. She must always find the gifts in the visits, what else can she hold on to?

May 25, 2000

Mom is combative every day, mostly with the male aides, but she chokes, scratches, hits, refuses, screams, and on and on. Every day or evening we get a call. It is immensely hard to see her or hear about her like this. The question poised in the air and then posed was, was she ever abused? It hung there waiting for an answer. No one knew. It shrouded the space around Mom and never will we know that piece. And now with it in our minds we wondered if, then, what then, how do we…..

I went there in the evening, this time to see this combative stuff, to see if I could help in some way. She was just fine until they had to get her ready for bed, changing her and putting her nightgown on. She struggled, but because I was there, it wasn't as bad. The aide was very gentle and quick, and the whole time she held on to my hand tightly not liking this at all, making all kinds of noises. I kept saying, "Mom, no one is going to hurt you, it's all right, I'm here, I won't let anyone hurt you." Quickly it was over, and I sat with her a long time, held her hand and prayed for her. When I left, she was sound asleep. She never had any more episodes of that kind of violent combativeness or struggle with help in dressing. Who else but God?

May 26, 2000 - Next chapter…next day.

There are times that the elevator ride seems too short and my feet feel like lead, like yesterday, but today was better, and I found the three ladies sitting on the couch outside the nurse's station window. I had brought a camera to try to capture the faces and personalities of the other women there. Mom had no problem posing. Happy and Hungry was ready and sat up straight for her picture. Racer said, "No," and sped off in her walker. Chirper just chirped as her shot was taken. Suddenly Racer, who ended up in the previous picture by accident came rolling over and said, "Do you see all these lights flashing?" I said, "Yes, I'm taking pictures." "Okay, as long as you see them too," said she.

The "town" was getting agitated. Ruth, nicknamed Spitter, was at the water fountain trying to get a drink, and every time she tried, her alarm went off. It's a string attached to an alarm so that every time someone tries to get up from a wheelchair it goes off, and the nurse would have to come and reattach it. Then Ruth would spit on the floor, not pleasant lady spits but craagh spits. I moved to different spots to avoid it, it was rather disconcerting to experience.

Mom was being fed by Elizabeth, an aide. Happy and Hungry looked like she hadn't stopped posing, and Racer was telling Elizabeth that she, Racer, might get her head bashed in if she said something. Elizabeth responded "Mabel, no, you won't, just say something." So, with tears in her eyes Racer said, "Well then my mother and my father." Elizabeth said, "Well, let's go back and look at their picture in your room," whereupon I watched as Racer and Mom trailed behind Elizabeth down the hall. Elizabeth can often be seen rocking the ladies, and they all come and take a turn on her ample lap.

It is difficult to write the not so nice stuff to you all, but it all is a part of it, thanks for following or letting me think you are..

May 27, 2000

I heard on the phone the other night that "Chicago Conley," which is how Mom likes to be known lately, had joined a gang. The gang consisted of Leather Gloves Shirley, Two Timer, and Chicago Conley. Well, this gang had decided to unlock an unlockable door, this particular door belonging to the bathroom where the tub is. They snuck in, and all three got in the tub, no easy feat, believe me, and had (in the nurse's words) a tête-à-tête. I didn't ask too many questions because I was busy laughing. That was a good night and one that does good for all of us. I try not to have any expectations of each day, just let it come as it will.

When I got off the elevator today, I noticed her door was closed. So, I peeked in, and one of the aides was helping her with her toileting. So, I gave them some privacy and waited outside. When at last they emerged, Mom grabbed my hand right away tightly and said that we needed to go walk. We didn't get too far before she saw Dad and said, "Nor, are you ready to go and fight?" I saw lots of red flags with that, what the heck did she mean? I was so hoping that it wasn't that she really wanted to go and fight. Heavens who was I kidding, I was talking about Chicago Conley. I saw her gang members in the distance watching us. I was hoping that they didn't have any plans of ambushing anyone. We had a nice visit, and she was pretty motivated. Most of her words were muffled and somewhat confused, but she could still wink and kid a bit, even if you didn't know what she was winking and kidding about. Trying to get into Mom's world is okay for about a minute, but anything deeper is too far beyond a rational mind.

Racer woke up and got afraid, and as usual raced over to us, "Hello, Mabel," I said. "What?" she said. I responded with, "I just wanted to say hello," whereupon she started to cry, "No, I don't want to be alone." I shook my head, touched her shoulder, "You aren't alone, Mabel." Then she said, "How come every time I see you I don't need anything from you?" What answer did I have? You guessed it, none. Every once in a while they stump me, and all I can do is shrug my shoulders and say, "Okay."

Happy and Hungry saw me and asked if I was good. I said I was and was she? Oh, yes, she was good, and they (whoever "they" were) had a good time. She also asked if Mom was good. Meanwhile I am hearing Leather Gloves and Two Timer whispering, "Her daughter has her now, and she's pulling her along." Mom was winking again and one finger waving to Leather Gloves and Two Timer. I felt a little like I was in the middle of the streets of Chicago, and I was being fingered and getting ready for the "ride."

Where was Singer? Sleeping a lot. I miss seeing her awake. As you can tell there's been some good days lately, fun days. Hope they stay for a while. The combination of medicines they have Mom on are doing what they need to do. Thankful for small and large gifts. Love, me.

May 30, 2000

Once I went to the third floor on a Sunday and saw Helen and her husband sitting in the dayroom. Helen, if you don't remember, is the lady I call Picker. She walks up to you, looks at you and cocks her head one way or the other. I have never really heard her talk. But here she was with her head on her husband's knee, and he was gently rubbing her back. It was very tender and sweet. They didn't say anything, just sat there. Again, I notice the touch. That's what's important, not really words, just a touch and familiarity.

Last night and today Mom did well. She ate and drank and took her medicines. Even though she has become Chicago Conley and is quite the feisty one, living up to the name I guess, she was pleasant and relatively quiet while I was there. When I came to get Dad, she was busy being busy with the ladies and walking about. She came over to Leather Gloves (who Mom has renamed the Queen) and sat down by her. Leather Gloves put her arm around Mom's head, and Mom laid her head on her shoulder, and Leather Gloves looked at me and said, "She likes doing that, I don't know why." Then she stroked Mom's cheek and said, "I love you, you are a little pet." Mom told her she loved her too, then looked at me and said, "She's the Queen." Well, that was the first I heard the name, and Leather Gloves said, "Well, I will have to go way high up there," which for some reason, unbeknownst to me, just cracked them up.

That's it, just taking one day at a time.

June 2, 2000

Mom is a lot weaker the last couple of days because of the medicines she has to take. In order to regulate her moodiness, there is this drug and that drug, and all of them tend to make her unsteady on her feet. So, often she sits in a wheelchair. It is not my Mom, who, once so vibrant and busy and such a good and steady walker, is now relegated to slow, shuffling steps. Her fierce independence and stubbornness are still there, and though it might cause problems for the nurses, it is still that part of her that she can hold on to. One almost, and I mean almost, has to cheer for that part she holds on to as if it is the last vestige of who she is. She still manages to recognize us, however, and I am glad of that. We are constantly working with the doctor and nurses, changing this medication and that one.

The other day she was sitting by her friend Singer and looked at Dad and said, "Where is Pop?" For those of you who don't know who Pop is, it is my father's father, and everyone called him Pop. Anyway, she said, "Where is Pop going?" Singer said "That isn't Pop, that's the egg man," to which Mom replied, "Oh, it is?"

I visited with a woman who was visiting her grandmother, and she was telling me that her grandmother used to be a meat packer and loved the Twins. The grandmother just kept saying, "The who?" Sigh.

Not too much more today. Well, there is, but there are times when even the writing of it is just too much to do. Love, Linda.

June 3, 2000

I don't often go at night to visit, but I did last night. Mom is very stooped lately and closes her eyes most of the time. She is a bit more awake and motivated in the day, but at night she is more like I described, stooped, eyes closed and seemingly one emotion, indifference. The nurses were busy changing her bandages, but she kept hiding the bandages and taking the old ones and hiding them in her clothes. Pretty interesting dance. All these ladies are so spunky. I wish you all could meet them. Leather Gloves told me in no uncertain terms that I was to stop combing Mom's hair, that it looked beautiful now, and that I should leave it alone or else she wouldn't have any anymore. She has quite a few opinions on every subject.

June 4, 2000

Mom has been falling quite a bit, scraping her arms with her paper thin skin. She was not opening her eyes today, so I had some time to look about me and observe the other ladies. Suddenly Racer came up and said in a sing-song voice, "I don't know your name, but I know your face, who are you, should I know you?" I told her my name, and she told me hers. It was such a normal thing to do, the mind doesn't forget everything.

I also saw a woman named Jane, whom I have called the Caregiver. She is always dressed very nicely and is such a soft spoken woman, and she always wants to know how people are and if they are all right. She is very complimentary to everyone. You think you would love to have a conversation with her, but what comes out are those wonderful encouraging things but nothing else that makes much sense. She is very caring and solicitous towards Mom. As I was watching Caregiver, Racer came up and said, "Are you folks having fun?" I hesitated for a second simply because I didn't know who she was talking to and then said, "Yes, we are" and she promptly sat down in her walker and said, "Well, I'm not." I laughed, and she smiled. She really does make me laugh. Laughter is a definite gift and must on that floor. Write later....me.

June 5, 2000 - Larry, Curly and Moe.

On one of the walks up the hall yesterday Mom walked into Picker's room. As I glanced around quickly, I saw a picture on Picker's wall. It was of her and her husband probably about 10 years before, and she was lovely. I mean really lovely, not that she doesn't have her own brand of loveliness now, but a real beauty. All over I am amazed at what this disease does to its occupants.

This morning I had to pick up Mom for a doctor's appointment. I saw Picker and Singer asleep on the love seat, Happy and Hungry was busy looking for food or fun, and Leather Gloves was trying to get away from Mom who was picking at her. Leather Gloves said, "I think that outside is a good place for her." Mom had her jeans overalls on and was getting lots of compliments from the other ladies, and so she was pretty pleased with herself.

I will tell you this tale from the doctor's office. I hope you can picture this. It is what my friend Shelby and I would call a "Shelby" or a "Linda," which really means a Three Stooges kind of situation.

Mom was pacing to and fro from one seat to the other in the examining room waiting for the doctor. She sat precariously on the table end, then slid off that and sat on the step that gets you up on the table. She didn't want shoes on when we left the nursing home so she came without shoes. Then she went to the round stool that doctors sit on and sat there, then back again to the table, and on and on, every once in a while saying, "Well, come on."

Well, finally the doctor comes in and notices that a bench needed to be moved because there were so many bodies in there. Mom was on the table sitting precariously again. Dad was standing around in the middle of the examining room, which as we all know is very small. Doctor says, "Norm, please move over there so I can move this bench." Now, all the rest happened at the same instant. The doctor starts to move the bench, Mom is suddenly sliding off the end of the table like butter, and I am trying to hold on to her so she doesn't get in the doctor's way, Dad is trying to get out of the way and tries to step over the round stool (why he wanted to step over it instead of around it is a mystery in itself), but as he lifted his leg to step over it, his foot landed on the stool, and it started to roll. He started hopping around on the other foot with his foot still on the stool. He was traveling pretty fast, and I could tell he just couldn't figure out how to get his foot off. Mom is continuously melting onto the floor, and the doctor is standing there with his mouth open and a horrified look on his face. Dad is looking at me as he is hopping around, he's now laughing, and by then so was I. Finally the doctor got him disengaged from the stool and said, "Norm, sit down there and don't move," which, of course, he obeyed, and then the doctor said, "Laura Mae, sit on that table," which, of course, she did not obey. However, order was restored, and I think the Doctor held in his laughter pretty well. Oh, my gosh, one of the funniest things I have seen. Totally Three Stooges.

The bottom line about Mom is that she has two other compression fractures in her upper back, exacerbated by the original site. She does not seem to be in pain, thankfully. It does, however, hamper her breathing, but again, thankfully, she is not heavy, that would make it that much worse. The ride back to the nursing home was uneventful. I kissed Mom goodbye, hugged and touched each one of the ladies that I know, and Dad and I went home. He was exhausted, but we laughed and talked about the doctor's office shenanigans the whole way. Love, me.

June 6, 2000

What a squirrelly day on the third floor. Surprisingly enough, Mom was the least squirrelly. In fact, she had a good day. She even was a bit more responsive. She had her pretty blue eyes open and looking about. She still is very unsteady on her feet and either rides in the wheelchair or pushes it as she walks. She even let me comb her hair. A good day. When I sang the song, "I Love you, Lord," she sang with me, all the words. A very good day.

As I walked and pushed Mom in the wheelchair up and down, suddenly everything, as I said, got squirrelly. Picker was busy taking her shirt off and didn't have anything on underneath, Spitter was spitting, and Two Timer dropped her full diaper on the floor saying, "I don't like it," walked over it and kept walking. Racer ran over it and got caught and couldn't move, and Caregiver came over, picked up the diaper saying, "What is this?" A janitor ran over and looked at me and said, "Get a nurse or an aide," he obviously couldn't leave. I did as he asked, telling the nurses, "There is poop all over the floor," which there was, trailing Two Timer, who by now was almost to her room. The aide came running. They got the diaper, put some paper on the floor where the stains were, and went to call another janitor. Suddenly one of the other ladies started picking up a piece of paper that was covering one of the places and started folding it. I took it and put it back on the floor when Happy and Hungry sidled up to me and got me engaged in a conversation about a phone book and that she needed to call some people. I managed to deter her thought and looked about for Mom, who was watching all this with cool detachment. The Boss lady kept saying, "What's going on," over and over, and Chirper, not to be outdone, woke up from her nap and started her bird chirping. All of a sudden, Dad, who had been down at the end of the hall where Two Timer was making her retreat, walked very fast past her and into the dayroom and said, "There is poop all over the hall and the floor, it's time to go," and he immediately ran to Mom's room to get his jacket, he had had enough for the day. I thought it was a good time to exit as well, we really were only in the way. Apparently, when you hang around there enough, you might see any number of things that you might not like. We had that kind of day today. I also saw one of the ladies pinch the rear end of one of the young male aides who was bending over to retrieve something from the cart. I felt like I was in the middle of yet another Three Stooges episode.

June 11, 2000

I have an update that is full of positives. Mom is good. Good means she is not combative. She is walking around and being Nurse Conley and helping the nurses on their rounds and being comforting when she can to the other ladies. Mom does not seem as angry as once she was. She seems to know me when I visit, and once when I asked her if she knew who I was, she said, "Of course, I know who you are." She is eating well and drinking again, and the infection that she had has cleared up. We are all relieved and so pleased. Singer and Leather Gloves were sitting together when I walked by, and I heard one of them say, "I don't like her," her being me, "I just don't like her." I had just been over there having a nice conversation with them, you just have to shake your head. Singer was really on today. She said that she was going home to heaven soon, and I should come with her. Ah, not yet!!

Good summer days, these.

June 14, 2000

There they were, the three of them, Singer, Chicago Conley and Leather Gloves. Mom was sandwiched between them on the love seat. It is after all a love seat, but somehow they sit there squished together. Picker is the other sandwich when Mom is not there. Two of the gang members, Leather Gloves and Singer, were having an argument, and Mom was listening very quietly watching Leather Gloves, she is a very animated person to watch.

Singer: "Your Mom and I are going to go up yonder to Heaven together, she said that we were going together."

Leather Gloves: "No, you aren't, I'm going."

Singer: "No, I am."

Leather Gloves: "No, I am, and besides God can't take more than one, so I'm going."

That pretty much ended it, but Mom was still watching Leather Gloves intently. Pretty soon Mom just got up and started walking. For awhile I was singing "When the Roll is called up Yonder" with Singer and Leather Gloves. We didn't get very far when back Mom came to the love seat and stood there. Leather Gloves reached for Mom's hand, which Mom took, and then said, "They all like me, I don't know why."

Mom and I walked the halls a lot. She goosed a couple of people but talked to most of the ones we saw.

I am going to take a quiet walk, will get back to you.

June 19, 2000

The conversation between Mom and Leather Gloves went something like this:

Leather Gloves: "Ouch! She stepped on my toe, the one that really hurts. They all pick at me all the time, she should go eat or something."

Me: "Well, Shirley, she already had lunch with you."

Leather Gloves: "Not with me, I haven't eaten yet."

Well, I never know what to say when they say stuff like that, so I just smiled like the Cheshire cat. Pretty soon she had changed her mind and Mom was her best friend. Have I ever told you what Leather Gloves looks like? She is a tiny woman, and her legs seem to start under her breast bone. She wears large glasses on her tiny face. She is missing one half of one of her fingers, which is probably why she wears gloves, and she has about ten rings on one finger of one hand. She is really cute and reminds me of one of those wonderful cartoon characters. She does have quite a personality.

As I looked, Mom and Dad were both awake just sitting together not talking. Mom is slouched down as usual because of her back and shoulders, and it looks like her stomach is perched on her chest, and she was just staring. I sat down and was watching the goings on. Caregiver was yelling for Racer to shut up and stop crying, that she would get dinner pretty soon. Of course, Racer wasn't asking for dinner, but Caregiver thought she was. Oh dear, now I'm trying to assume what they are thinking, how scary is that?

The angry woman I told you about a while ago rarely comes out of her room. She still seems very angry at her husband and won't talk to him most of the time. He tried not coming one day, and then the next time he came she was angry because he didn't come, and he said, "Well, you didn't talk to me last time," their voices trailing away. It must be so hard for them both.

Racer managed to find me and ask me if I would take her to the bathroom, she had to go really bad. I steered her quickly to the nurse and then she looked at me as if to say, I don't have to go, what's wrong with you. They are so tricky, makes ya think!!

June 20, 2000

I stepped off the elevator and looked in the usual places, which means the hallway and dayroom. They weren't there. I stopped to say hello to Happy and Hungry, who was immediately complimentary about my dress. I said hello to Leather Gloves and Singer, who was sleeping, and Racer. I stood there a minute trying to figure out where they were and looked behind me into the dayroom, and there they were looking at me in a quizzical way, maybe they thought I was just another patient. As I walked over to them, Mom held out her hand with a half smile on her face. I sat on the floor by her legs, and she reached for my hand. It seems that this is the most comfort to Mom, to hold someone's hand, and at this point it actually doesn't seem to matter whose.

We all watched then. Chirper was in the alcove sitting across from Spitter. Chirper was busy chirping, and Spitter was busy shaking her head in a manner that seemed to say she was incorrigible, and she is. I watched as Picker started across the floor towards us, picking at her top and pants. She stood there in front of me staring at me looking as if she wanted to say something. She stuck her finger in her mouth for awhile, and then she took my hand and held it for a minute and walked off. Pretty soon Janet, a new lady, looked at Picker and said, "She doesn't make very good conversation." Janet is the lady who came up to Laura one time and touched her hair and told her she liked her worms (it was most traumatic for Laura). All of a sudden up zoomed Racer, who said, "How will I know where you are?" I said, "Mabel, I'm right here," and she said, "No, you aren't" and zoomed off. Back she came in a minute and said, "Will I find my way?" I just nodded my head, yes, and she said, "Why are you shaking your head?" I laughed and said, "You caught me," and off she went.

Some of the ladies were watching Lassie, and Chirper was chirping very loudly, and Caregiver was saying, "She is impossible, and I wish she would be quiet." Soon the nurse wheeled Chirper away, and as she was being wheeled away, she sang out, "I can still see it." Now imagine bird calls and squeaks here.

In the corner there were two ladies. One of them was in a recliner, and the other was in front of her in a wheelchair.

The lady in the wheelchair was very intent on getting the other lady's slipper off. She picked and pulled, and after many minutes, she got it off, and then after equally as many minutes, she got the other one off. If any of you remember the Pirates of the Caribbean ride at Disneyland, this next thing reminded me of it. The wheelchair lady, now having gotten the slippers off, started pulling on the tights the lady had on. She took hold of the toe and started pulling. When she had about a foot pulled out, the recliner lady pulled it back up, and that would start it all over again. They did this back and forth without stopping. Once in a while the recliner lady would pull her foot away, and then the wheelchair lady would grab her foot as if it were a fish out of water. Dad and I just watched and laughed. Once the wheelchair lady looked over at me and waved and then went back to her task. No sound, no words were passed between the two.

Racer caught me and said, "Please help me stand up so I can get my wits about me." I told her I would get a nurse and to please just sit there. When the nurse came and inquired what the problem was, you guessed it, some poop misery. The nurse said she would return shortly with her walker and left me there with Racer, who was still trying to get up and wincing each time. Now I am sweating. I'm expecting at any moment poop to fly out, and I kept saying, "Mabel, it's okay," when clearly it wasn't and, "pretty soon someone will come." I thought of flapping my arms but didn't think it would do any good. Finally, an aide came, and off they went. I sat down by Mom, and she said, "Now, they're giving her the one, two, three." I said, "What's that?" She smirked and said, "If you don't know, I'm not telling." I thought I better quit while I was ahead.

The wheelchair lady never did get the tights off while I was there but was still trying when I left. Racer was much more comfortable, Lassie was still on, Chirper was chirping, and Spitter was about to spit on the floor.

A young nurse told me today that this was her dream job. She loved working with these ladies and felt that she somehow helped and made a difference for people when she went home at night. We are very thankful for all the nurses and aides like this one.

June 23, 2000 - Mini tales from the third floor.

As I write, Dad is standing by the front door waiting for the senior bus to come and pick him up. True to his nature, he is ready at least an hour ahead of time and will always be seen waiting, watching for whomever.

Things are quiet on the third floor. Yesterday I had extra time and wanted to take Mom outside to walk a bit and get away from the third floor. But when I arrived, Mom was asleep, a deep sleep. I didn't want to wake her up because I know she is busy all night pacing about, and sleep is something she needs, but I was disappointed. It seems every time I have a bit of extra time she is asleep. In fact, most of the ladies were asleep in varying poses and places. One of the aides and I started talking and walking as I made my rounds.

Dad feeds Mom everyday and gets an aide to change her. He is very faithful to his task. It has given him a purpose to be able to continue in any capacity to care for Mom. He is always looking for her shoes, which end up in other people's rooms, one or both. However, he forgets that she is also wearing slippers that aren't hers. I think they are Picker's since she is the one who wears this type of slipper. It frustrates Dad since he feels that things should rationally stay in Mom's room, but then the third floor isn't a rational place.

It seems that I rarely write about things when they are quiet, and in truth, often on the floor things are quiet or the ladies are asleep. I went to the support group they have, about six of us were there. I listened and shared and realized that they all sound alike, differing stages of combativeness, cursing, odd dressing, sundowning, all the terms I am becoming quite familiar with. I also noticed that laughter was the order of the day in the group. As you know, I laugh a lot on that floor.

When Mom is feisty or angry or sleepier than usual, I don't experience a lot of sadness, but when she is more rational (and there are still times when she is, albeit briefly) and she smiles at me or sings with me and allows me to give her a kiss, then I am quite sad and moved to tears. The other day she was like this. I told her I had to leave, and she said "Goodbye, I love you," turned to Dad and said, "Just touch me and say you love me." As we walked to the elevator, I turned to look at Mom, and she had turned her attention away from us and was just starting to get up from the chair, and I knew what she would do, resume her walking up and down the hall, back and forth, waiting I assume for the next thing, or perhaps when she does that, she is waiting for when Dad will come back. I don't even know if she remembers that we were there. It seems as if it's automatic, when we leave, she is up and pacing. There are many joys in spite of the disease, but, oh, so many sorrows.

June 24, 2000

Mom was awake, and they were sitting at the end of the hall. Dad had his usual harem, All Day Sucker and Worms were sitting or standing and staring at him. As I approached,

Mom said, "I recognized you," and I could tell that she was truly glad and was surprised that she did. That tells me that she doesn't always recognize me, and it explains the quizzical look I see on her face at times. We took a long walk outside today. It was hot with a nice breeze, and we sat on a porch swing and swung our feet for a long time. I combed her hair, and she mentioned that the birds in the grass were pretty. They were really just shadows, but I could imagine with her. We sat in silence most of the time, and sometimes I thought she was saying something, and when I bent over to try to hear, I couldn't make it out. Finally, she wanted to just walk, and so we did all the way to the end of the driveway and then turned around to come back, but she was tired and starting to lean forward more and more, and then she was taking mincing steps and walking faster and leaning over more, and I was wondering how in Heaven's name I was going to hold her up. I considered screaming but figured I would scare everyone including Mom, so that was out. By now we were mincing so fast (I was mincing along with her, I could do nothing else) that I was out of breath. At long last we made it to the door. We shuffled in place for a minute or two, and then we were back in the elevator going towards the third floor. She was clearly out of breath but seemed to have had a good time. I was exhausted!

Dad was pacing, waiting for us. He had forgotten where we had gone. The harem was gone, and so we sat Mom down next to Singer on the love seat. Mom immediately put her head on Singer's shoulder, who harrumphed at her. The ladies do a lot of harrumphing and honking at each other. Anyway, Mom sat there for a minute and then this conversation ensued:

Me: "Mom, would you like the plum I brought for you?"

Mom: "Okay."

She proceeds to eat it with great relish, in fact, with such gusto that she was out of breath, and the juice is squirting all over the place, but she is definitely enjoying it.

Dad: (Speaking to Singer) "Did you have plums in your yard?"

Singer: "What?"

Dad: "Did you have plums in your yard?"

Singer: "No, I didn't have any bums in my yard."

Dad: "What?"

Singer: (Looking at me) "He thinks I had bums in my yard."

Mom: "Ha, ha, ha."

Mom is cracking up at Singer's statement about bums, while she's eating her plum.

Singer: "I had plums, and once in a while I had bums, but I always helped them out with a pitchfork."

More laughter from Mom who is still enjoying the plum. Dad gave up after the "what" from Singer.

I saw Racer. I kind of steered clear of her since she looked like she was in a panic again, and it would seem that the only time I see her in a panic is when she is in, ahem, "distress." I saw Leather Gloves as we passed by, and that is where we left Mom and her friends, enjoying a plum, thinking about bums, and laughing. Just before we got on the elevator one of the aides stopped by, and in our conversation I mentioned that I write about the ladies on the third floor. She was intrigued and mentioned that I should tell you all that she is the best. She is very cute, looks about 16, but is probably in her 30s. She always has a smile on her face, and clearly Dad likes her perkiness.

And Dad? Dad is fine except he lost the basement tonight. It took him a while to find it. Today was a good day. Love, me.

June 25, 2000

I do hope that I can remember all I want to remember today. The ladies were all very squirrelly today, or perhaps I was squirrelly, and they were normal. You be the judge.

Dad was sound asleep with his mouth wide open, and Mom was busy tying and untying her shoe. I passed ladies in the dayroom. They were all there in a little knot. Mom decided she wanted to walk, so we started down the hall. Two Timer met us, and fortunately, this wasn't a diaper dropping day. Mom steered me to the love seat where Singer was asleep and Leather Gloves was looking about. As soon as we approached, Leather Gloves said, "No, no, I don't want her over here by me, she pinned my arms so hard that I couldn't breathe, and she scratched my eyes out." Considering what had happened weeks or was it months ago, I wondered, and so I asked a nurse. No, she hadn't. Good news. We continued on and came across Chirper who was in full force chirping.

We stopped, and Mom said hello to her, and Chirper said, "No, you can't ask me any questions." Mom said, "Well, when you ask a question, you're supposed to answer." Chirper said, "No, I don't." As we walked away Chirper said, "And a peeter deeter deeter to you." Mom said, "What?" I repeated it, and she said, "Oh, yeah?" I thought I better steer Mom away and let Chirper keep chirping. We stopped and sat down close to Leather Gloves who promptly said to no one in particular that the lady in blue (that would be me) she didn't like, and she was going to kick her. I just stayed where I was trying to blend in. Leather Gloves was trying to wake Singer up when suddenly

Singer said quite loudly to Leather Gloves, "Go back to the city you dumb sh…" Mom asked what she said, I repeated it mostly and said, "But she is talking to Shirley not to you," and Mom said with a mad face, "Oh, yeah, same thing." In the next few seconds Caregiver crooked her finger at me and said, "Come here, Missy, I have something to show you." I smiled weakly and looked at Mom and said, "What do you think she wants to show me?" Mom smiled and said, "Wouldn't you like to know." Well, actually, no, I didn't want to know at all, but what I said was, "We have peeter deeter over there, now Jane wants to show me something that I am sure I don't want to see and Shirley wants to kick me." About then Mom is thinking this is all pretty funny, but at least today no poop issues.

From then on Mom was not together in her conversation. It was kind of all over the place. She asked me why I hadn't come to see her four times, no answer to that. Then she told me that she had talked to her Mom. When I asked where she was, the answer was, "She went to the east." That ended that story. She also told me she remembered us, that is, Susan, George and I, when we were around 12 (does that mean we were 12 at the same time), and that we were very misbehaved kids. Well, what could one say to that? I tell you a squirrelly day on the third floor.

Leather Gloves' son told me that she had been a waitress for most of her adult life, and I bet she was a good one. When she heard her son telling me that, she wanted to know why it was my business, which, of course, she was right it wasn't, but that launched her into Mom pinning her arms down, etc.

And Dad? Tonight he went to bed at 5:00, got up at 6:00, got dressed, and no matter how many times Don and I gently say that it is night and that he probably will want to go back to bed, he isn't getting it. I do hope you all are praying for us still because we need it. And I pray for all of you too. Thank you.

June 29, 2000

It was a beautiful day for Mom and Dad's 61st wedding anniversary. The kind of day that is a perfect Midwest summer day. Everything is green (we have had plenty of rain) and warm, not humid, and just enough breeze to cool you off if you get too warm. The sky looks like it is painted on a canvas, blue, blue, with fluffy white clouds. Dad kept saying over and over how beautiful the sky was and how he just couldn't get over it. We were on our way to the nursing home, and I was driving him there because the senior transportation either forgot, or I got my date mixed up. I wasn't able to stay and have a visit then but would come later and visit when I picked him up.

A few hours later back at the nursing home I stepped off the elevator and looked down the halls at either end. They were there at the end that has two chairs and a table in between. To get there I have to go by the dayroom and the love seat by the nurse's station. I had two pieces of anniversary cake and a camera, hoping to get a picture of them on their special day. Our friends were all there, Leather Gloves, Singer, Caregiver and even Happy and Hungry, all sitting in a little knot. I spoke to them all, touching them as I passed by. Leather Gloves said how nice it was for me to visit, and Singer asked me if I knew her daughter, and I told her that I had met her once. She asked me if I knew where she was. I responded that I would tell her that her mother was looking for her. As I neared the end of the hall, I saw a woman sitting on the table. As I got closer I recognized the senior companion who used to visit Mom at home. And then I saw Mom with her cut off jeans, tennis shoes and white socks, she was very cute. Her hair was a little wild, but then all the ladies' hair is in some state of disarray most of the time. Mom was in good humor the whole time I was there. We talked about The Boss. We talked about some lady who has a tail on (you got me), but Mom thought that was extremely funny. Then we laughed about peeter deeter deeter, which surprisingly Mom remembered. I showed her the two pieces of cake I had brought, and she promptly ate them both at the same time, no hesitation about using her fingers, frosting all over and crumbs on the rug. She enjoyed and posed for the picture nicely. No one really came over to visit us, and that was just fine. We had a nice time of laughter and memories. It was time to leave, so I said another Happy Anniversary, left Dad to say his goodbyes, and as I was walking down the hall, the janitor, who was then walking towards me, put his hands on his hips and said "I have no idea what I came up here for, I think I better take a room." I know how he feels. I walked to the elevator, and Singer yelled out, "Aren't you going to get the pills for my legs?" Leather Gloves was saying how nice it was for me to visit again, and Chirper said, "Are you leaving already?" A nice day on the third floor, and as we drove home, Dad broke the silence with, "I just can't get over that beautiful sky." A nice day all around. Happy Anniversary, Mom and Dad.

June 30, 2000

I had a nice visit with Chirper's granddaughter......

Actually, I had started this update, and Dad came upstairs with his time warp, and I need to sit and talk to him. If anyone has any wisdom for Dad, I would appreciate it. Thanks…love you all.

Dad is settled again. As I was saying, I had a nice visit with Chirper's granddaughter. I found out that Chirper carried twins that died in infancy. She worked in many jobs doing whatever she could to help out. She had perfect pitch as a young woman, which is probably why she loves to chirp all the time, and she is 83. The granddaughter converted to Catholicism, and when I said I was Catholic, Mom looked at me so shocked and said, "You're Catholic? I don't like that." She was just so frustrated with that news, but she couldn't really say why. That passed, and we went for a walk.

I do not know what to do about Dad. He suspects conspiracy in everything, trying to tie totally unrelated things into one huge ring of whatever his mind has concocted. I listened to him for an hour tonight. It must be so hard to be so confused. I tried to name some of his fears for him, and he agreed even to the conspiracy theory, but because he thinks I am a part of it, it doesn't help. He is afraid that he is crazy (he isn't), and I suggested that it sounded like he was just being paranoid, and there was nothing I could do to allay his fears in this area. I suggested talking to the doctor, but he is hesitant because apparently the doctor might be in on the conspiracy. However, I do think he will talk to him, but I don't think it will be the healing he hopes for. I don't think it will just go away, his dementia will eventually pull it out again. I know that God's grace is sufficient, but I am so not equipped to deal with these kinds of things. I can bandage it for a night, but it drains me and saps my energy. Keep praying!

July 2, 2000

I haven't seen Mom for two days, and I wondered if she would know that. She didn't. In fact, she was asleep on Dad's shoulder and just grunted a hello. When I asked the nurse why she was so sleepy at this time of day, she told me that Mom had had an agitated night.

I didn't just want to go home. I felt like I needed to visit somebody, but I can't really tell you why. The ladies were quiet, several of them spoke to me, and I met a new lady on the floor who was very glad to meet me. Maybe I like visiting the other ladies because in some way this connects me to Mom. Dad said that when he tried to get Mom to walk with him, she got feisty, but when an aide came over, she went just fine. Dad was amazed. He didn't get it, and neither did I.

I am having trouble writing tonight, my mind is all tumbled about, I feel kind of foggy. I hope that you can glean something from this that will make sense.

July 3, 2000

I cannot believe I have failed to mention that Mom is now on Hospice. It was frightening to me at first, that word. Hospice and death seem to be synonymous in my vocabulary, but as I learned, it isn't necessarily so. Susan was here when Hospice talked to us the first time. We both just wanted to cry the whole time, and then we didn't want to, and so we didn't, but we really wanted to and were perpetually on the verge of it. They are very caring and tender, and that made us want to cry too. They asked if we would like a music therapist, and we said, "Yes." Mom loved music and made that a part of our lives, and we felt that she would enjoy that. Dad came home one day after this young man had come and sang with them. Dad was glowing and sharing how wonderful it was and what a nice young man he was.

One day, and this is what got me thinking that I hadn't shared about Hospice, I was up there when the therapist was there, and I tell you Dad was so right. He has such a soothing, wonderful voice, and he was very tender with both of them, particularly Mom. I sang along with them after he had picked songs with some help from Mom. It was like all those years of Mom playing the piano and Susan and I singing along. I do hope there will be another time I am able to be there to join in the singing.

So, I don't just associate Hospice with dying anymore. There is a lot of love and caring and helping, maybe death, but not just death. I think it must be a requirement that if you work for Hospice you have to be tender.

July 4, 2000 - Happy 4th of July.

I should have known the minute I stepped off the elevator that something was different. Something not quite right for this place. As I looked to the right I was struck by the ladies in a very tight knot by the nurse's station. Most of the time they are in a loose circle, but not this afternoon, they were close together, quiet, with an occasional outburst from Chirper. I looked to the left and saw Mom and Dad. He only had an undershirt on top, and Mom was leaning against him fast asleep. As we walked down the hall, Donny asked me what that smell was. I said it smelled like someone had died (sheesh, like I would know), and just as we reached Mom and Dad, Dad said, "Two people died on this floor today."

It didn't seem like Mom was going to wake up, and we weren't able to stay long, so I walked to the nurse's station to let them know we were leaving since Mom needs more watching of late. I saw and spoke to several of the ladies that were there.

Racer seemed to recognize me right away. One might think this is a good thing, and it is to a point, however, I do not know what to do with her when she reaches out to me at times. She puts me in a quandary. She wants to sit, then stand, then turn around and have me go with her. I got her turned around and then walked back toward Mom and Dad, who was just then getting up to leave.

As I got in the elevator, Racer was walking by and said, "Where are you?" I said, "Right here, you are fine." She said, "NO, I'm not." And I had nothing to say back to her. So, I waved goodbye, and off she went.

It has been two days of sleepiness with Mom, and I recognize that any awake connection for me is important, more so than I realized. I hope that tomorrow is different.

July 5, 2000 - Halitosis.

This will be short. Lately everyone in my family has been telling me I have bad breath. Apparently my breath was backing up on the third floor yesterday, perhaps that was the smell that we all thought was death. No one died on the third floor yesterday. Someone did die on the second floor but all were accounted for on the third.

It wasn't a bad day, a busy day, but not a bad day. I hope that my bad breath doesn't waft out over the e-waves at you. Good grief. I think I can't listen to Dad anymore when he tells me these things.

July 6, 2000

It was yet another squirrelly day today on the third floor. The nurse thought that it was because of the noise from the large vacuum and dryer they use on the floor. I don't know, but even Mom was affected by something, and, no, it was not my bad breath. Mom was irritable and watched everyone and didn't seem to want to go anywhere or do anything. She just wanted to stay in the dayroom and observe.

Chirper was clearly in charge today. Not only did she chirp non stop (annoying everyone, especially Mom), but for some reason she was going after Racer. Every time Racer started traveling anywhere near Chirper, she was angrily telling her that she couldn't go that way, that she needed to go another way. Racer would just stand there and start to cry, and then she would be allowed to go. I got up to ask the nurse something, and Racer called out "Susan," which is the name she has given me. I answer to it simply because she gets very upset with herself if I don't. She needed me to disengage her from someone's wheelchair. Chirper asked Dad if he thought he was some big shot. Dad didn't answer, but she kept calling out after him. He doesn't really like being in the dayroom, I think it's just too hard for him, but Mom wanted to stay. Mom seemed distant and confused. She told Dad that if he left, he wouldn't find her tomorrow morning.

I don't know a lot these days. It's easier to write about the other ladies, the same ache isn't there in my heart even though I genuinely like them all. I don't know if the days on the third floor are getting harder or what, but I know that I have to gear up for it. Perhaps knowing them has made it harder to comprehend that one day they won't be there. A lot of thoughts roll around in my head.

July 9, 2000

I found out today that Racer is really 89, that she and her husband never had their own children, so they adopted two boys. She is a tiny woman with a very pixyish face. Her hair is white, and she has sparkling blue eyes. She wears hearing aids, which are always falling out, and that makes it almost impossible for her to hear.

They had a cellist there today who was playing for his grandmother, and we all were the recipients of his musical ability. He was very good!

July 12, 2000

I was met by Racer yesterday when I stepped off the elevator. I looked up and down the hall and didn't see Mom or Dad. Suddenly Racer was there.

Racer: "I was wondering when I would see you again."

Me: "Well, here I am."

Racer: "Well, it's about time, where've you been?"

I think I am in trouble, this might be one of <u>those</u> conversations.

Me: "Well, I have been here."

Racer: "No, you haven't."

See what I mean?

Me: "Well, I guess I will have to come see you more often."

Racer: "Well, that is better, I like that."

As I turned to walk away from her looking for Mom and Dad, Racer suddenly called, "Linda." I was so surprised. I had told her my name once, and even though she has been calling me Susan, I guess this time it registered. I walked back to her, and she said that she hoped I would come and visit her again. I promised I would see her soon.

Mom seemed distant and detached again today, closed eyes, didn't want to hold my hand, didn't want to sing. Sigh.

These moods are hard to experience. As we were walking, Chirper chirped out a hello. Mom waved her away as if to say, oh, puke, which is Mom's favorite phrase lately.

It is cyclical lately with my visits and my emotions. I pray on the way up the elevator, and I pray on the way down. I might not write for a few days unless there is something really funny or uplifting. Right now I feel as if there once was a veil covering my eyes so all I would see were the funny things, and for some reason it is gone. Perhaps when it comes back and I can mostly see the funny stuff again, I will be able to write more. Love you.

July 17, 2000

I remember when the kids were little, and they would take one of my fingers and hold on tightly, usually associated with walking somewhere, but yesterday Mom was busy eating an apple and holding on to my finger very tightly. I liked it. She has been tired still of late because at night she is agitated and not sleeping. Susan and I are going to do a bit of sleuthing at the home. We want to go and observe Mom for a little while, hopefully, unobserved ourselves, to see how she is at night. She apparently is very different at night than during the day. And after we spy on her, hopefully, we will have a nice visit with her. I let the nurses know what we were planning. Though they looked a bit strangely at me, they had no problem with it. Of course, I will tell you all about it.

As I was standing with Mom, suddenly I heard a sound like a whinny over and over and over, it seemed to go on for 20 minutes. It is a woman whom I have not seen too much, and I don't know what the problem is with her, but I have heard it before. It is her unique cry. There are the most interesting manifestations with this disease, each one individual and unique.

Lots of love here tonight. Mom is in a good place.

July 19, 2000

Enter Stage Left: Mom and I walking down the hall, where else, you might ask.

The Boss: "Are you the dentist, the new one?"

Mom: "No."

The Boss: "Well, I need my tooth worked on. When are you going to get to it?"

Mom: "I don't know."

The Boss: "Well, I think that this is a terrible way to run your office."

Mom: "So what."

We continue to walk down the hall.

Mom: "She is a pistol."

Me: "Yep, she is."

She steers me over to Leather Gloves and Singer.

Me: "Well, you guys aren't pistols."

Leather Gloves: "We aren't what?"

Singer: "What, pickles?"

Me: "No, pistols."

Singer: "No, I don't want any pickles."

Leather Gloves: "She said pistols. What are they?"

Singer: (Loudly) "NO, I don't have any pickles."

Me: "Okay."

Mom is going through yet another thing, I'm not sure what, but she seems afraid, you can see it in her face. She is afraid of the ladies and the people who work there. I sat with her on the bed for a bit, and she was so tired. In fact, she was so tired that she almost cried, and she kept saying that she was afraid. I asked her of what and she said, "Solidity." Then she said, "Linda, I am sorry about us." The nurses say that she is very afraid and sticks to them like glue, and so they hold her hand, whomever is handy, up and down on their rounds. I had to get an aide to come and sit with Mom when I had to leave yesterday. It was very sad, and we both were full of tears. She couldn't remember her maiden name yesterday. I can only wonder what is happening now.

And The Boss? She crabbed about the dentist the whole time I was there. She shook her fist at the nurse's station, and she and Mom had a little tussle about who was first. Mom won, pretty cute. Racer was sitting in a funny way in her chair sound asleep. When I showed Mom, Mom said, "Don't point." Once a mom always a mom. Smile. Love, me.

July 25, 2000

Susan and I and the kids went to Valparaiso. We had a great time. We played cards, laughed a lot, did some visiting with our cousins Don and Carol, and also visited friends of Mom and Dad's.

The night before we left, Susan and I went on our spy adventure. We sat at the end of the hall and could see Mom in the distance walking about with her nightgown on. By the way, we absolutely saw nothing except Mom walking about with her nightgown on and once in a while speaking to someone or stopping to look at something. After about 15 minutes she started walking down the hall towards us. We just kept sitting there being dorky. We kept saying, "Okay, this is so dorky." When Mom was closer, we called to her. She looked at us, but I don't think she knew who we were. Susan was convinced Mom didn't know her, I am not sure at all, and we will never know. For all we know, Mom was trying to ignore us and knew who we were right away. But she allowed us to take her to her room, where we tucked her in, and then she held on tightly to Susan's hand, and it wasn't until she was fast asleep that we were finally able to leave. It was sad for Susan, she hadn't seen Mom for a while. We both talked about when we were little and Mom and Dad would play cards with friends, how we loved listening to the chatter and clatter of cards being shuffled, and pretty soon we were lulled to sleep by their voices.

Susan has gone, and, of course, now we have humid weather and thunderstorms, all things she was hoping to experience. I miss her already. So, I am back online. I have no idea where this will go or where it will end. I am glad you are all in it with me. With love.

July 27, 2000 - Tales from the turd floor.

Mom had woken up when I got there and was ready to walk. I had brought an album of old pictures of when we were kids, and we sat and looked at it. She kept closing it when we would get to a place where the pictures were ones where we were much older. She couldn't remember them, and then she would say she didn't like it. I have seen that kind of frustration on the other ladies' faces. They get angry with themselves at times when they can't remember something. It must be incredibly disheartening for them.

As Mom and I were walking, Two Timer walked towards us and started her funny repeating word sentences. We stood there and listened for quite a while, mostly because this is the first time that she has talked at length with me, and I didn't want to leave her when she was so animated. However, once she was done, she continued on, and so did we.

We turned around and caught up with Dad, who was walking slowly behind us, and now the three of us were walking together. Soon we came upon Two Timer again who was standing at one of the doors and saying, "I have to pee, I have to pee." I suggested she go ask a nurse, which definitely brightened her up. And so we continued. Pretty soon we met up with her again, and this time she was breaking up a piece of candy, chocolate, a small one, and dropping it on the floor. Dad picked up a piece and asked me if it was a turd. I was suspicious and said, "Drop it, Dad." As I looked back at Two Timer, I could see that this is exactly what it was. He saw too, and for the rest of the time down the hall he was holding his hand like surgeons do when they are preparing for surgery. He kept watching it closely. Finally he said, "I think I need to go wash my hand." I agreed, but we laughed about it anyway. If you are wondering why it took so long for him to wash his hand, the hall is long, and he had to get somewhere to get to a bathroom.

July 29, 2000

There is definitely something about Two Timer and problems with her bowels. There was another incident on Friday, something about stuff on shoes, everyone's shoes. Racer was having trouble remembering where she was, Picker was busy on all fours racing after some dogs who were there visiting, all the ladies loved them.

Mom has two sleepy days and then one animated one. She shuffles a lot when she is walking. She forgets what she's doing and shuffles in place. Then when she remembers how funny it looks, she starts laughing. Some of the ladies look a bit beat up. Mom had a couple of dings on her arms, Leather Gloves had a scratch on her face, Racer had a bruise on her cheek and her lip had a couple of bumps, wonder what happened?

The woman who was always so angry with her husband was up yesterday in a wheelchair, and her husband didn't look quite so distressed. I am so glad for them.

They now have a man on the floor, as in patient, presumably waiting for a bed on another floor. There are only women on the third floor. They definitely segregate the men and women. He only has one leg, and I guess they figured he wouldn't give the ladies a hard time. Not much happening right now on the third floor. Quiet is good.

July 31, 2000

All the beds are filled on the floor. It is amazing to see so many ladies. There are still so many that stay in bed or hide out in their rooms. Really I only see about one third at any given time. Today there were a few who I hadn't seen before sitting in the dayroom. The usual ladies were scrunched in the love seat under the nurse's window. It seems that Leather Gloves owns all the chairs in the place. Once, Mom, Dad and I were sitting in the love seat in the dayroom, and I waved at Leather Gloves, who could be heard saying, "That's my seat, why are they sitting over there?" As little as she is, I wonder how she can commandeer all those places, but run it she does. Racer was Racer. She caught me and said, "Where is Linda?" I said, "I am right here," (she had <u>me</u> wondering for a minute), then she said, "Are you sure?" Eek. Then she mentioned that she was a throwback, to which I said, "Oh, no, you aren't." Soon that got turned into, "I have to throw up," EEK!! And in the next breath she said, "No, I'm all right." Talk about running the gamut of emotions and flight responses. I told her that I was visiting my Mom, and she said she wished she had one to give me. I didn't see the lone male. He may have gotten scared off with so many ladies on the floor.

Mom says she forgets what she is doing, and that's why she shuffles. She leads with her head and so is constantly in danger of toppling over. Dad doesn't really know how to hold her and walk with her. He tends to pull her along, which makes it worse for both of them. It is an interesting thing. She starts out fine, and then all of a sudden she is shuffling in place.

I brought a candy for her today, and like the plum, she ate it with great relish!

As Dad and I were leaving, a priest came up to the floor and blessed the ladies. He made the rounds and talked to them in a gentle voice, and he made sure he touched all the ladies' arms and shoulders. The three of us ended up on the elevator together, and Dad asked him to pray for Mom. So, he stopped the elevator, prayed right there, blessed us and continued on our ride. Perfect! Love, Linda.

August 3, 2000

I have noticed something just recently. Mom stands or sits in place until she is given some direction to do something or other. She stood up, and I asked her what she wanted to do, and she said, "I don't know, whatever you want me to do." She was just waiting. That, too, is an incredibly sad thing for me to see, and yet I am sure it is a blessing to the nurses and perhaps for Mom too. It just seems her independence is fading bit by bit. As I have said before, she seems more animated with the staff than with Dad or myself or any visitor that comes. I am glad she feels that connection, but I miss my Mom lately, miss being able to share with her, miss seeing her awake. Perhaps I need to find a different time to visit.

Dad has been told that he might have Alzheimer's. He is on a medication to offset some of the problems he was having. He is sad but stoic and continues his faithful vigil at the nursing home.

Racer still calls my name, Singer liked my clothes, Leather Gloves looked a bit upset, All Day Sucker has been very angry of late, and Happy and Hungry was searching on the snack cart for more ice cream, and they were all congregated around the nurse's station, except those, like Mom, who were asleep. I really missed her today. Love, Linda.

August 4, 2000

I changed my time today and went to the nursing home early, and she was wide awake, and Dad was sound asleep. I brought grapes. One of the ladies was reaching out her hand for some, and fortunately, I had some foresight and thought this might happen. Mom enjoyed them as well, but she did have trouble getting them off the stems.

I took her for a walk outside in her wheelchair. At first she didn't want to go, but I persuaded her gently, and off we went. She was very adamant about what she did and did not want to do and about what I should or should not do. It was nice to see some of her old stubbornness and independence back for however long. I wasn't even sure I would be able to get her back inside when it was time. However, the problem wasn't getting her inside the "university" (Mom's word) but on the elevator. She flailed her arms on to the sides of the elevator, planted her feet and said, "No, we are not going on this." So, we walked up and down the first floor hallway, and who should we see but Happy and Hungry. I asked her what she was doing down here, and she responded that she had no idea, she was just waiting. As it turns out, she is moving to the second floor because the level of her Alzheimer's is not as far advanced, if you will, as the other ladies on the third floor. I will miss her. They are also thinking of switching Leather Gloves, but ...well, I guess I don't know enough about it. However, I got Mom back on the third floor, she just needed a distraction.

Racer was a throwback today (her word). She was having another one of those days and kept telling Jude, one of Mom's favorite aides there, that he better stay where she could see him. So, every time we walked by him, I said he was in trouble with Racer. The ladies all like him. He has a very nice smile and is very gentle with them. I offered Racer some grapes, but she said I should put them in an envelope and mail them to her.

I enjoyed the visit today. Mom refuses to look at me when I am doing something she doesn't like, but that doesn't matter, I, at least, got to see her awake and talking.

August 7, 2000

I stepped off the elevator and looked about wondering if I would find them in the usual places. Just the other day I couldn't find them in all the usual places and finally found them in a room sound asleep.

However, I looked around and saw them at the end of the hall with a wheelchair in front of Mom. As I approached, Mom said she didn't know who I was, and then "Norm" told her who I was. We walked a lot today and spoke to the ladies who were sitting about. Racer was doing her usual thing of calling me to help her and come and talk to her. I did and then sat her down or stood her up as she was requesting. We saw Picker today too. She hasn't been in the dayroom too much lately.

Some music was on, and I asked Mom if she wanted to dance with me. She said she would. So, we stood up and moved our feet for a minute. June, The Boss, was having a wonderful time watching us in spite of her all too obvious black eye and was smiling at our attempts to dance. Picker even was moving to the beat. Mom was perky today, and while I love that, it also makes me sad because it is harder to leave her. She is obviously disappointed when we have to go. As we left, I was dancing toward Leather Gloves and Singer when true to form Racer comes flying up, and Leather Gloves said, "Why don't you just sit down and be quiet." Racer said, "That's all right for you to say, you just sit around like a bump on a log." Even as I write, I am shaking my head and laughing.

The nurse said Mom has made a new friend, a new lady on the floor. The other night she found them sitting on a bed chatting away.

It would seem that it is an endless stream of too much medicine and then not enough and then not the right kind and on and on, not just for Mom but for all of them. How difficult it must be to live that way having medicines control your behavior. In spite of it, the human spirit is strong. I see it in the ladies. In spite of the disease, they are alive in there. I may not be able to communicate well with them, but they are there. I wish I could tell you about everything I see, but it would take too long and fill too many pages.

Alas, Dad is mixed up in his sleeping patterns again. I hope tonight is a turning point. Love, Linda.

August 9, 2000

It is getting harder for me to write these updates, not because things are necessarily harder at the nursing home or even here, but because my world is so small right now. There is this darkness that descends on me once in a while, not to be confused with depression, but a darkness. It's like a blanket that I can't seem to get out from under. Of course, at these times prayer is the best lifter of it, but I usually smother for awhile before I remember to pray.

On this floor the ladies are pretty much relegated to traveling up and down two halls and occasionally in their bedroom or someone else's. I watch. They are looking, always looking. When they are sitting, they have no idea what they are looking at. This is how my world feels for a small moment, the house, the same travel route to the nursing home, the house, a doctor visit, etc. Perhaps the sameness is the darkness, as in the case for the ladies on the third floor. It is a perspective, a small one, I grant, of how they might feel.

They were at the end of the hallway. Dad was dozing, and Mom was awake and perky. I asked her where she liked to be the best and she said, "In the middle," which would be the dayroom. Dad spirits her away to the end of the hall when he is there, partly for aloneness, but also because it is too hard for him with all the commotion with the ladies. Mom enters in when she sits in the dayroom and isolates herself when she sits at the end of either hall.

As I hugged Mom goodbye, I said, "See you later, alligator," and didn't really expect an answer, but she said quite clearly, "After while, crocodile." I walked to Racer to say goodbye, and when she saw me, she called out my name. A lady who was talking to her said, "Oh, that's Linda? Now do I look like a

Linda?" Racer said, "I don't even know what one looks like." Really, how does someone, number one, keep from giggling and, number two, have an answer for that? She says those kinds of things every day, I just can't always remember them.

The lady that is always so angry with her husband? She continues to be in the dayroom but will not speak to him the whole time he is there. She just sits and stares and won't swallow her food while he's there. Yesterday he sat and talked to her. When it was time for him to go, he said goodbye, he would see her tomorrow, and he walked out of the room. No response from her. I hope he does not feel too defeated, it would be a hollow victory for his wife if she is trying to punish him. His faithfulness in coming in the face of that is commendable. Of course, I am only seeing one small part of a much bigger picture.

August 12, 2000

Dad didn't want to go to the nursing home today, but I went because I knew he would feel better if someone did. Mom was asleep, so I sat there for a few minutes and then took a walk in the hallway until she woke up. I spoke to the gang in the alcove on the love seat, touched Racer as she raced by, and went back in the room. She was awake by now and looked at me quizzically. I asked her if she knew who I was, and she said she didn't, who was I? She looked long and hard and said, "Susan." We sat on the love seat that had been vacated, and as I talked and she listened, she was looking hard at me. I asked her if she remembered when Mother V and she and I went to San Francisco and rode on the cable car, and did she remember that she jumped off early, and Mother V was afraid that I would jump off too, and then she would be lost. So, she jumped off and bounced on the street and rolled, her wig flew off and stopped at the feet of two Asian men whose eyes were wide with horror? Mom just cracked up. She says that she does remember that one, it is one of her favorite stories. Even when she didn't have Alzheimer's, she and I loved retelling it to each other and anyone else who would listen. I told her that she was a good mother, and that I loved her. She said, "I was? I am glad you think so." She didn't ask about Dad. Neither times or days seem to mean much there. I stayed for a while longer, kissed her goodbye, and told her I would be back tomorrow. "Tomorrow?" she said. Sometimes I think it must seem like one long day to her.

Dad is having some bizarre behavior, he is not making sense. I will have to call the doctor on Monday and see if he can make sense out of nonsense.

Tears were ever present today. Love you all.

August 15, 2000

My hair today was windblown, and I really mean windblown. I looked like Pippi Longstockings without the pigtails, my hair sticking straight out from my head. I got off the elevator and started looking around for Mom (it was my day to visit today), and I didn't see her anywhere. She wasn't in the dayroom or the end of the hall or even in her room. I asked Jude, and he said, "She was around here somewhere." Just as I was passing The Boss, she said to me, "Look at this, she, (Racer) just went by and bumped into me." Suddenly she looked at my hair and said loudly, "Hair, hair, all this hair, it is just going everywhere, this hair." Well, I will tell you it took all my self control not to laugh out loud and long. I found Mom finally and took her outside for a long walk and time on the swing. We literally said nothing, we just walked and/or swung. Mom said, "I enjoyed my day today." "Me too, Mom."

Leather Gloves wanted to know if I was the Mom, and I said, "No, I am the daughter." Leather Gloves slapped Mom on the knee and said, "Well, you stinker, how did you do that?" Racer said she was sorry for hurting my simples, and I said, "That's okay." I just never know what she will say…smile.

August 17, 2000

It is hard getting used to this new way of visiting Mom. Dad and I are alternating days. Except for the days that he doesn't go and thinks he went, it is working in a way. Today was the second time for my visit, and I was hoping she would still be in that conversational mood. She was glad to see me and was ready for anything. So, we took a long walk, even longer than the first one. I noticed that she stared straight ahead. Even though there was much beauty on the walk, there was very little that she took notice of, or at least she had nothing to say about any of it. Her talk was a bit on the odd side today, odder than usual. She kind of had that wild eyed look that I see in Racer especially, but I see it in the other ladies too at times. When I walked to the elevator to go, she held on to my shirt so I couldn't go. So, I walked a bit more with her and had to get Jude to help me distract her so I could leave.

She fell tonight and has a big gash over her eye and one on her arm. This was the report we got, and they have no idea how she fell, but she apparently looks pretty beat up.

Leather Gloves and Singer were off today too. Leather Gloves' son was there, and she wouldn't let him go, and Singer was mad at Mom and me today.

Oh, well, moodiness was the reigning emotion of the day. Love, me.

August 21, 2000 - Marching to a new beat.

Don and I got off the elevator and looked about. We were told that she was walking around somewhere. There she was down at the end of the hall hugging the wall, tentatively walking, looking very frightened. She recognized Don right away, and as I wheeled a chair to her, she reached out for me. We headed outside waving to Leather Gloves and Singer, with Leather Gloves saying "We haven't seen you in a long time." We strolled Mom a long way with Don pushing and Mom holding my hand, silent except for an occasional "Can you see that, Laura Mae?" from Don. We sat on a bench for a short time, but even outside Mom either wants to keep going or sleep. It's the same with Racer, running, going, going, going. We walked as far as we could. As we turned to go back, Mom wanted to walk, so Don held on to her, as he described it, kind of like they were doing some strange dance. She was snuggled into his chest and held on for dear life. I finally walked behind them pushing the chair, and pretty soon Mom's steps got smaller and choppier, and pretty soon Don's steps matched her mincing steps, but sounding like two wooden marionettes marching to some silent drumbeat but totally in unison. It was slow, painfully, hilariously slow. I wanted to laugh so badly, but I just couldn't. It just didn't seem like it would be taken well by Mom. I look like that too with Mom at times when I walk with her. It is quite comical. Finally Don said, "Let's sit down," and put her in the chair, and a fresh wave of controlled laughter bubbled up because Don was just dripping sweat in spite of the cool air.

Back on the floor we sat Mom down in the alcove by the other ladies, who all seemed in rare form today. They were all glad to see each other. As I commented on the lovely tea they were having, I kissed Mom goodbye, Don did as well, and this time Mom was content to stay with the ladies. Sometimes the ladies reject each other, and you would think that wouldn't matter, but even now it does. Today these ladies were basking in each other's acceptance. Nice.

August 22, 2000

It was my day again, and as I stepped off the elevator, I noticed Mom right away sitting in a chair in the area where the nurse's station is. She recognized me immediately and looked so glad to see me. She didn't get up, however, and very quickly I found out why. She is just too frightened to walk and won't even try without help. Mom and I sat and listened to Leather Gloves, Singer and Chirper for awhile. She spoke once and said, "I wish I were dead." When I reminded her that it was in the Lord's time, she said, "I know." We sat and observed, but that wasn't different, she and Dad always enjoyed watching people. Chirper was busy chirping without her teeth, which was even funnier. Finally, I got Mom up to walk, and after a few tries she started walking, and then she was fine, but only if I would hold on to her.

Today Picker came by and actually smiled, and it was a lovely smile. You know the saying the eyes are the window of the soul? Hazel's soul must be lovely and warm and kind and loving if her eyes were any indication. For the first time with me she made eye contact, and she smiled. What a gift today.

Mom's new friends seem to be Chirper, Caregiver, Racer and Picker. Quite an interesting group of friends she has.

Today she wanted me to read to her from the Bible. Not for long, but I read, and soon she was asleep, and I left.

Dad is having trouble with being afraid to go places because he's afraid he will have an accident like he did at the nursing home a week ago. So, he isn't eating all that much, I guess figuring that the less he eats, the less comes out. One cannot reason with an aging parent when they get their mind set on something. I feel like my parents are folding, and I am back and forth between them trying to do what? Be a gatekeeper? Make this transition as painless and loving as possible? I probably need to get out of the way and just let the Lord be in charge. All I need to do is be loving and kind and pray.........a lot. Love, me

August 24, 2000

I went to the nursing home yesterday with Tasha, my niece. She is beautiful and blonde, and the women were enthralled with her. New blood as it were. Caregiver rolled over in her walker, Two Timer started talking, and Leather Gloves, yes, Leather Gloves got up from her love seat and came over and sat down. Never had I seen so much attention paid to someone, it was very cute. Mom was standing when I got off the elevator, but I noticed a chair right behind her. She has a chair close by her now. The nurses do that because she is very scary when she walks lately. We visited, sort of, Mom doing her stare, maybe she is trying to remember something and perhaps staring helps. Mom didn't like the fact that I was talking to Leather Gloves and kept giving me the stink eye, which, of course, made me laugh and then made her smile, but the visit was difficult at best.

Dad also is having a new problem with going there besides the fear of an accident. His new fear is that Mom will fall when he walks with her, which is a good thing to be cautious about and logical. I am afraid walking with her at times as well. So, he is contemplating going only once a week. He sleeps a lot. A lot.

One thing that Leather Gloves said was that Mom is making a fist cause she is getting ready to hit me. That's when Mom gave me the stink eye. Who knows, maybe Mom is queen of the roost there. Just kidding, but then if Survivor is a game of life, surely this third floor is a game of life of sorts.

Oh, yes, Racer was asleep again, I miss her calling my name.

August 31, 2000

Mom fell again, smashed her face on the tile floor and had to go back to the hospital ER for stitches. I went today with Dad. She doesn't look as bad as I thought she would. However, she is in a wheelchair with a lap buddy on to keep her in there. It is sad. She keeps wanting to get up and can't. She did eat for us, Dad fed her, but she wouldn't look at me. Finally, I asked her if she knew me. She said, "Aren't you the same?" I said, "Yes, the same Linda." For the most part she answers questions pretty clearly, but when she is just talking, you can't always understand her, nor does she make eye contact much. However, she did eat and held our hands. That at least is something.

I don't know what to say about Mom. It seems that it is a matter of changing meds to control things that your body used to control when you were young. Now Mom has meds for everything, and the body just continues to wear down. Perhaps

I will have a funny for you next time. Lately there have been only sad things, or else I don't have eyes to see the humor.

September 1, 2000

Yesterday we were there at the lunch hour. I am not usually there during a meal. In fact, I normally avoid it, partly because it often can be gross, and partly because I am hesitant to feed Mom, and here I was, right as they were serving lunch. Even with the hacking, spitting and stuff falling out of people's mouths, if I could just look at it as if I were feeding a child, then perhaps it would not seem quite as hard to do. Mom eats fine most of the time, but there are so many others that don't. Some of the food is pureed, and others liquefied. All Day Sucker was busy drinking and spilling her pear sauce down her bib, Racer wasn't eating, and some, like Mom, enjoy the food but don't always remember what to do with the utensils. They didn't have enough aides to feed everyone in a slow manner, so lunch was rather hurried to make room for the next group to eat.

I have noticed that many of the family members that come to visit their loved one do as I do and stop and touch or visit some of the other ladies on the floor. Mom is often included in their rounds, and how glad that made me.

We do not go today, and I know that Dad will forget that we are going every other day, but he will have to abide by his plan and my availability. We will call, however, and perhaps next week he will want to go back to the original plan of going every day. But today is today, and tomorrow has enough troubles of its own. Love, me.

September 3, 2000 - Tales from the almost "turd" floor.

I know, what can I say? It seems as if there is always some kind of poop story.

Yesterday Dad and I went together to see Mom. We had had such a good report about her the night before. Apparently the change in medications has helped her quite a bit, and we were looking forward to more of the same when we visited. Mom was in the dayroom in the wheelchair with the lap buddy, and she was moving the wheelchair around with her feet. It seems this maneuvering is kind of an instinctual reaction with everyone who has to spend time in the chair. Right away she knew us, and her face lit up when she heard our voices. She doesn't make great eye contact, and she speaks in a mumbling way, but every once in a while she would say something quite clearly and appropriately. Her face is now two toned, one side green and the other normal. Her wounds are healing, we are thankful for that.

I spent some time walking up and down the hall with different errands, one for the brush to brush Mom's hair, another for something else. On the way back on one of the trips Racer spied me. So, I went over and said hello to her. She said hello back and then tried to say something else in her stuttering and halting manner and suddenly said, "Poop." That was my cue, "Well, Mabel," I said, "I will see you later." I walked away and then about two minutes later I could hear her "Liiiinda." I looked over and saw she was stuck with her hearing aids dangling and went to help. It just makes it that much harder to talk to her without speaking loudly because she really can't hear without them and not much with them.

Mom does not have the same problem with us leaving lately. She says goodbye easily. Susan always said that Mom was a trooper, that she adapted to wherever she was. She is right, Mom does. That's a wonderful trait.

September 5, 2000 - Tales from the third floor and assorted things.

When I go and visit the grandkids, one of the things I want is for them to recognize me right away, especially the babies. Yesterday when Dad and I arrived at the nursing home, we noticed an aide talking to Mom, and as we got closer we could hear him trying in vain to get her to recognize him. He is one of her favorites, and he had been out of town for a couple of weeks, and unfortunately, she did not know him. I could tell he was disappointed that she had forgotten who he was. I am like that with Mom and am afraid that one day she will not remember who I am, and that's why I keep asking her if she knows me. I am also like that with Racer. I will be disappointed when she does not remember my name or who I am. We all like to be recognized and remembered by people we care about, whether it's babies or the elderly who have dementia, wonder what that is all about?

Today was Mom's checkup day at the doctor's. As usual I picked her up, not as easy anymore with her not walking very well or not at all. We wheeled her out in the wheelchair, and she did okay getting in the car. She would not raise her head to look outside. Whether she didn't want to or couldn't, I don't know, but she didn't and held on to my hand tightly. If I told you every time I cried, I would sound quite pitiful, but know that many times tears are right there ready to fall at any moment. This was one of them. While we were waiting to be called, she would stand up and sit down, up and down, over and over.

She can't stand by herself anymore. Someone has to hold her up, and it isn't easy, she topples over and can't seem to stand straight enough to have any balance. The doctor said he didn't know if the deterioration in certain areas was due to the disease or the compression fractures. It might be both, so he will continue to watch. As we left, I couldn't get Mom into the car. Literally, she was sitting on my hands, and I had no clue how to get her in. Dad, meanwhile, was running back and forth getting wheelchairs and bringing them out to the car and then saying, "Linda, oh, that isn't you," and I would say, "Yes, it is" and back he would go to get another wheelchair until finally I said, "Dad, I don't need a wheelchair, I need you to go get a nurse, I need someone to help me get Mom in the car." Off he went, and I was hoping that he would bring someone. Thankfully, he did, and with some effort we got her in. I don't know if something that happened was funny to Mom, but on the trip back to the nursing home she started to smile. Dad is just hilarious!

It seemed that today she didn't always know who I was, and several times she said, "Oh, it's you." To which I would say, "Yep, it is, Mom, just me." Love, me.

September 12, 2000

It seems ages since I have written. Busy is an excuse, but truthfully, I have not wanted to write. However, writing to you all has been such a cathartic thing for me, and again I thank you for reading and laughing and sharing it all with us.

Mom was in her room today, Dad was with me on this visit. He kept trying to run me over with the wheelchair because he would forget that I was sitting on the floor in front of Mom so I could look at her and talk to her. She keeps her head down and doesn't look up very well. She is much more lethargic lately and looks so much like a lost little girl. Her eating isn't good either, and the nurses will call the doctor if she does not perk up soon. She still reaches out for my hand if I am kneeling down in front of her so she can see me, and she looks long and hard at my face. And when I say, "I love you, Mom," she still says, "And I love you," in a whisper.

I heard All Day Sucker talk today, actually she yelled. One of the other ladies came over to her and touched her arm, and she yelled, "You don't know nothing, just shut up." Everyone looked around and was shocked to hear her.

They moved the love seat from under the window by the nurse's station to the dayroom and even though Leather Gloves and Singer still sit there, they aren't liking it. In fact, it has so discombobulated them that they are having trouble talking to me and figuring out who I am. It doesn't take too much to get them confused. Routine is best on the third floor.

There is a new lady on the floor, and she, too, has one of those lap buddies. She takes it off every five seconds. One of the nurses counted 100 times while she watched. She doesn't seem to try to get up, just wants to take it off. She tried to get Dad to help her today, that's when he was busy trying to run me over. Mom thought that was funny, it made her smile. It wasn't much, but it was something.

September 15, 2000 - Assorted tales times two.

That times two is nurse talk. I am learning their lingo or trying to. It has gotten cooler here of late, and this morning instead of Dad's usual tan shirt and tan pants, he put on a plaid flannel shirt and tan pants. As Dad was pushing Mom past the ladies in the dayroom, suddenly Leather Gloves leaned over to Singer, I think she was trying to whisper, and said, "I told you he was FBI."

Today when I asked Racer how she was doing, she said, "Not very damn well, thank you." This is how the day started with the ladies on the third floor. They are doing a new thing with the meal times. The ladies that can still feed themselves go down to the main dining room for their meals. This means less aides that have to take over that duty with the ladies who are not able to feed themselves. I think the ladies are confused by this and can be seen milling around the elevator and looking like they want to escape. Racer asked Jude if they were going to kill her. I would say they were a bit confused today.

Tonight they were confused as well. I went to see Mom by myself tonight. I didn't see her as I got off the elevator. One of the nurses said that she was in the television room. It's a little room off the hall, but I have never seen her in there before. She and four other ladies were watching some television show. We sat, she stared, I talked, and she held my hand very tightly. She ate some ice cream that I fed her, she thought I was Susan, and she said she couldn't think.

Susan asked me a few days ago if I was ready to let her go. I wasn't sure then and am still not sure I have an answer. As I was driving home, I thought about it and realized that though I don't know that piece yet of letting her go, there is still something I think I need from Mom. Whatever it is, I am guessing it is a selfish need for affirmation, and in her present state that is not something she is able to give. But tonight as I was talking to Mom, she said very clearly, "You have to let me go." Could she have been talking about the very thing I had been thinking about? Probably not, but my answer and the only answer I could think of giving was, "Yes, Mom, I will let you go."

I needed to leave, and as I pried my hand from Mom, I hugged her and kissed her cheek. I walked out of the room and met Picker who took hold of my skirt and stretched it, just as Caregiver rode up saying, "I have to get past, I have to go, ooh, I am not going to make it." At the same time all that was happening the nurse was busy telling me some things about Mom, while Racer was rolling up behind Picker and couldn't get past her because now we had this strange thing bottling up the works. Racer is saying, "What girl, why is everyone against me?" Caregiver is still pressing the point that she has to go, why won't I let her go. I am still trying to extricate my skirt from Picker, and Picker is holding on tightly, and now there is another woman saying, "Go, girl, you go, girl," (I am not kidding either), she was saying that to Picker. While this was all going on, Singer, who is across the room, is waving to me and saying, "Yoo hoo, yoo hoo." I waved, but she kept waving me to come over to her, but I was stuck and couldn't get free. All of a sudden, Picker let go, and things loosened up a bit. I walked over to Singer who took my hand and said, "Please talk to me, I have no where to sleep tonight. They told me that they had no room for me. Is it night?" I told her that I was sure they would find a room for her, but that wasn't enough. She was beside herself thinking that they had no room for her. I was rescued by one of the nurses who said that she was going to stay with her tonight. Singer was very happy to hear that!

On the ride down in the elevator a new aide said, "I will never get to know them," I smiled and said, "Oh, yes, you will."

September 24, 2000

Several days of not feeling well have kept me from visiting as much as I would like.

Mom stares, that is mostly what she does. While at times it is unnerving, sometimes I can look into her eyes and see that she is still there, it is just hidden from the rest of us.

Chirper threw a cup and a plate at Dad and cursed him out. He stared at her, and she stopped talking. Two Timer came toward Dad and dropped her diaper and said, "Want some?" No wonder he hasn't liked going and staying for long periods of time lately. I think Dad is a bit scared of the ladies. Two Timer is mean to him, seems not to like men, and she always has some issue with her diaper, and he has no idea what the rest of them are going to do or say.

Mom lost her wedding ring. I hope we find it.

September 26, 2000

I could see Dad was pushing Mom down the hall, so I stopped and spoke to Singer and Leather Gloves. Leather Gloves wanted to know where we were going. I said I was going to visit my Mom. The rest went like this:

Leather Gloves: "Who is your Mom?"

Me: "Laura Mae"

Leather Gloves: "Where is she?"

Me: "Down the hall."

Leather Gloves: "What's a hall?"

Now I was in trouble.

Me: "So, Shirley, I'll see you later."

Leather Gloves: "Bring your Mom here so I can meet her."

Singer: "Nice to see you."

Mom was sitting slouched down in the chair and staring, not at me, just staring. She didn't know me. She kept asking me who I was. She finally did remember after a half an hour and called my name. I do not know how I will feel when she never remembers who I am. Well, I can't go there yet.

As we were sitting there, Chirper was busy taunting Two Timer by singing and annoying her. Finally, Two Timer yelled, "STOP," then came running back to Chirper and slapped at her, at which point Jude ran over and intercepted any more smacks. Chirper just kept singing and saying she didn't do anything. It was a hard day for Two Timer. Jude just kept shaking his head. He is very patient with them all. He is working here to get through school, and he works very hard.

Speaking of men, there is a new man on the floor. He follows Dad around and asks him what to do. Heavens, Dad hardly knows what to do himself, but I saw the new man today sitting talking to Caregiver, it was cute. The other day Dad said that the little man dropped his pants, I guess it was a diaper thing again, glad that I wasn't there. I think I have this invisible sign on me that says, make sure you mention or have something to do with poop when you see me. Chirper today was singing her sing-song, and suddenly as I walked by, she snaked her hand like she was going to bite me and said, "Poop." See?

Racer doesn't seem to know me anymore. She talks to me but no longer says my name. It was kind of a coming home day. I am not even sure what I mean, it's just a feeling. Love, me.

September 26, 2000

I have been thinking of how to write this all day. It was a crazy day on the third floor, and Mom missed it or at least the part that I saw.

The two usual ladies were on the love seat, it is under the window again, and Picker was trying to squeeze in the middle of them and waking Singer up, which Singer doesn't like. Suddenly Two Timer shouted at me and came running over. I got a bit scared. She is an imposing large woman. Then just as quickly she stopped and asked me if I talked to her. I knew she was talking about Chirper, who was busy annoying her. They are quite a pair. Anyway, I spoke quietly to Two Timer trying to deflect the frustration she had going on with Chirper. Pretty soon Singer yelled "Stop it," to Two Timer. I asked what was wrong, and she said, "She's nuts." Two Timer didn't stop. She was busy yelling at a new man on the floor who was being led around by one of the ladies. She seems to have possessed him. She calls him Richard and then Ed and then whomever she can think of. He answers to them all and follows her around most closely. I am not sure how his or her family will feel about this, but it was cute nonetheless. Two Timer kept yelling at him to move, and he kept saying, "I'm trying to, but I can't." It was a little raucous there today.

After talking with one of the aides, I decided that one day a week I will come in the evening to visit. Mom goes to sleep right after lunch, and then she is out for several hours. When that happens, I sit with her, pray for her, remember things she did with us when we were kids, all those special things, whisper them to her and then give her a kiss, tell her I love her and leave.

I would say that Mom is at peace. She <u>has</u> always been a trooper, and she fought this for a bit, but she is at peace, or so it seems. We really have taken a back seat in her life. That has its sadness, but when I look at the overall picture, I don't dwell on that fact. It is nice to see Mom and not have to worry about her except to wash her face or comb her hair occasionally. I looked about the room today and felt like I was visiting "Mom's home," and it is. She has her little pictures about, the things that tell her and us who she is and was once.

Singer said something to me in Norwegian that meant "Those who sleep don't sin." I liked that. She did too.

October 1, 2000 - A short trip.

I close my eyes and once more see the lonely, almost eerie road in southeastern Oregon. The road went on and on seemingly with no end as if I was in an episode of Twilight Zone, and every mile I traveled, the road just kept getting longer and longer. The mountains in the distance never got any closer, I hadn't seen a car in two hours. There were roads that turned off the highway, but I couldn't see any signs that they would take me anywhere closer to civilization either. I never saw any markers or signs that made me think that I was getting somewhere, nothing. The wildness of the area and the endlessness of the road made me feel small and panicky, and yet I had a choice. I could retrace my steps, or I could take one of the roads and see where they led, and eventually one of them would have found a place that looked familiar. I imagine that this might be what some or all of the women on the third floor feel. In their minds they are on this road that doesn't seem to get anywhere, there are no familiar markers of anything, only roads that go off somewhere, but they don't know where they lead. A lonely, eerie feeling. They know that they are supposed to be somewhere, there is something out there, but there is no end to this wildness and loneliness.

Today I went to see Mom in the morning. She was awake and seemed glad to see me. Richard, the man in the previous e-mail, walked up behind us and stopped and stared. Mom reached out her hand, and he took it briefly and then let it drop. He just stayed there, and I could tell he had no clue what to do next. Pretty soon he picked up Mom's cracker, put it in her view, and when she didn't respond, he said, "Maybe she wants me to pet her." And so he did. He petted her hand very tenderly. As he was doing this, I asked him how he was and he said, "Well, I have to check my water still." Well, oh-kay.

Two Timer and Chirper fight all the time now. Two Timer swears, and then Chirper starts in on her. It has gotten pretty bad, and it tires everyone out. Leather Gloves was dancing with me to a Tina Turner song, and Singer didn't have her teeth in and had no idea where she was going, which was actually to lunch. It was a busy day on the third floor, but thankfully, no poop. Love, me

October 5, 2000

Susan and I watched Mom in the game time at the home. Singer was on today. As she watched, but didn't participate, she thought that every time someone did something right in the game, she was voting for the right person, and it might have been Truman. She even called her favorite friend Leather Gloves, a poop, and then would laugh. She was very funny really. Mom was not very with it, but she tried and seemed to enjoy the fun. It is always fun to go to the third floor with Susan!!

October 10, 2000

There are so many funny stories from the third floor. As Susan and I were sitting on the bed in Mom's room, I leaned over and said, "Can you imagine me trying to remember all of these funny things?" She said I was right, there was no way. I can't remember them all, and even if I did, I can't always tell them the way they happen.

There are days when Mom seems at death's door, and then in the next two days she is perky, smiling and doing so much better, which, of course, makes my emotions go up and down like a roller coaster. It was easier to handle with Susan here. We would walk around like Siamese twins that spoke at the same time. It was pretty funny. We were looking like we belonged there.

Dad thinks he's 42 and that it is 1985, and I wonder what will happen to him. Leather Gloves' son visits often and noticed that his mother calls Dad Don, and I can tell he doesn't like it. He wants people to know his name not someone else's. Sheesh, I am drained. Love you.

October 12, 2000 - Tales and such.

Two Timer said, "I poop, I pooped at 10, and I will poop." Really she did.

I was there this morning early. Mom recognizes my face but seems to have no clue who I might be to her. She didn't know my name and didn't really recognize it when she heard it, but we still had a nice visit. I left amidst tears.

October 15, 2000 - Tales and thoughts from the third floor

I can't imagine not thinking of <u>anything</u>. Thoughts, scenes, memories, daydreams, random threads run through my mind all day. I can't imagine being a contemplative, I can't quiet my mind for very long at a time. There always seems to be something scampering across my brain. Yet Dad and Mom and the women and man on the third floor seem not to think of anything, at least anything that they can hold on to and say, ah, this is it. Even Dad isn't actively thinking much. Dementia, like Alzheimer's, does seem to make a mind not only less active but erases so much. That is a curse, and I suppose in some odd way it can be a blessing. The disease is horrible, and yet at the same time the ladies don't know that it is horrible.

I saw Singer pushing Leather Gloves in the wheelchair today. Leather Gloves said it had been years since she had seen me, and Singer just wanted to know what to do with the chair. I saw Mom and Racer hold hands for a long time, really tenderly. So sweet to see.

October 17, 2000 - Tales from home.

I haven't been to the third floor in a couple of days, not because I didn't want to, but there have been pressing things here that I needed to take care of. I think I could start writing updates about Dad. The dementia is definitely worse. Today for the umpteenth time he thinks that the IRS is doing something to his bank account. Today for the first time I decided against trying logic and let myself into his paranoia, oh, scary thought. I told him that I would pray that he would find the problem, and that I was sure he would be able to find it. It worked, it calmed him. Even though the problem is not gone, he was appeased. What is actually unreal is a very big reality to him. I will try that again. I am glad that it made a difference with him. And then I called Susan and screamed in the phone. Love, me.

October 19, 2000 - Tales from the first, second and third floor.

As I noted before, people who come often to visit, visit not just their loved one, but others as well. The more one gets involved with the people there, it makes it all seem much more familial than just a last stop before death.

Richard is making himself known lately. Yesterday Leather Gloves was busy giving him Kleenexes, and he was just as busy folding them one-by-one. Leather Gloves commented on how nicely he was folding them.

When we got off on the third floor yesterday, there was Happy and Hungry. She was confused and had somehow gotten on the elevator on the second floor and just waited till the elevator stopped, and off she went. It was nice to see her anyway. As I was visiting Mom, kneeling in front of her, one of the nurses walked up and asked if she had a visitor. Mom, of course, said, "No." I did wonder what that makes me, but when she was asked who it was in front of her, she said, "Susan." Susan thinks she's making points with Mom, I think she is right.

It seems that there is a rash of wheelchair sitters today. I saw Leather Gloves and Singer in one. Singer was asleep in hers, and Leather Gloves, as I said, was busy doing Kleenexes.

An update on Racer. She is the same. I asked her yesterday how she was, and her response was, "Awful as hell." She pointed to me and said, "Linda's sister." I think Susan is making points with her too. Worms told Dad yesterday that I was her sister. Do I get a point? Love, pointless me.

October 25, 2000

It was my day to visit Mom. Dad isn't feeling well, but even if he were, it would still have been my day. I decided to go early in the morning again, that seemed to work so well before. As I stepped off the elevator, I could see lots of ladies in the dayroom, and unlike several months ago, no longer is Mom hiding in her room or at the end of the halls. She is out and about with the other ladies or with the nurses. I scanned the ladies in the dayroom, looked in the alcove, and didn't see her. As I was turning the corner to go down the hall to her room, I heard, "Liiinda, Liiinda." I knew it was Mom's voice, but it was coming from the dayroom that I had just looked in. I saw a woman waving at me, and I tell you unless she had been waving, it would have taken me several minutes to see that it was Mom. The only thing that was different was that she had a baseball cap on. It was pulled low over her face, and believe it or not, it changed her entire appearance. At best, it was so out of character for her that it just didn't register in my brain. What does that say about perceptions that we have of people we have known so well over the years? It is still a mystery how such a simple thing as a cap could alter her appearance, at least for me. The other odd thing is that normally Mom can't remember my name, nor does she really even talk anymore or certainly doesn't around me. Hmm, maybe there is something in that cap. Aside from mumbling that she was glad to see me, nothing more was said.

There was a lady there who was praying for the ladies who wanted prayer and could verbalize what they wanted prayer for, but she was praying over them all as best she could. She really had them quiet and listening, and that was good. One of the things she said was, "The Lord has their whole attention now, and even though it doesn't seem like it to the outside world, He is very busy inside each one of them." I liked that. She ended by going around to each one and touching and blessing them.

After she had gone, Mom actually sang with me and remembered all the words to the song she loves. All of a sudden there was a cacophony of sound. It started small, a gibber here and there, All Day Sucker started clapping and doing her sing-song thing, someone started coughing a terrible racking cough, Chirper was busy talking to herself, Mom was saying "Poor people," and on and on. It was like a wave of noise that started way back in the sea, and as it roared to the beach, it got louder and louder until it crashed on the sand.

One of the men who comes almost daily to sit with his wife leaned over to Chirper and said, "Hi, buddy, here is a present for you," and he gave her a Kit-Kat bar. He told her he had brought it from California. When he left, she rolled her eyes, and I could hear her mutter, "Who the heck is that? His name must be chocolate, humph." Then she smiled and clucked her tongue. Even Dad would have been amused.

October 27, 2000

Dad and I visited only for a short time today. We had several doctor's appointments. One of the social directors was busy entertaining the ladies. They all got into the act with some form of singing. Mom was asleep but seemed to have no trouble being in the room. Chirper knew all the words, I watched her sing them quietly. Music seems to be a wonderful calmer, and it doesn't need an introduction.

October 29, 2000

I went today by myself, Dad was busy at church. I sat and fed Mom her lunch. Picker was sitting down at the table, and the nurse turned her back for a moment to seat other ladies. Suddenly we looked, and there was Picker with her face in her plate. When she lifted her head up, it was full of mashed potatoes and gravy with bits of corn and carrots stuck to various parts of her face and hair. One can only giggle, which we did very discreetly, but truly she is the funniest dear little lady. Love, me.

November 3, 2000

Leather Gloves fell out of her wheelchair and fractured her hip. She is in the hospital and apparently in a few days will be back on the third floor. That seems to be the most common thing that plagues them, broken something or other. Singer has a new love seat partner, Richard, who was asleep on her shoulder. I think Leather Gloves will have to take her rightful place back when she returns.

November 11, 2000

Being on the floor with Mom in spite of her disease holds some real charm for me. No one tells me how silly I'm being or gives me instructions on how to do something better or tells me that they don't have time for me or tells me that things are undone and need doing or are embarrassed when I get ditzy. No matter who I stop and talk to they either would have all the time in the world to visit or not, and they might even walk away in short order, but they would appreciate the touch and time and smile.

Wouldn't it be something if we all would have more time for each other without an agenda? Love you all.

Sometime in November

Dear me, how do I start this one? Dad is up most every night and thinks it is morning, or he is up knocking on our bedroom door telling me about all the people who are in his room, and I must come and see right then. I am more tired than I know, and I think something must happen. And because of his increasing confusion, he can no longer go to the nursing home by himself. He is needing too much watching, and the nurses and aides don't have the time to watch him also.

I talked to the doctor, and he suggested bringing him in for a checkup and a talk. As he was talking to Dad about general things, he suggested that this would be a good time to talk about doing something else. I had to step outside, and as much as I try hard not to cry, I couldn't help it this time. I felt like such a bad daughter, like I had failed him, incredibly sad and like I had betrayed my Dad. Finally the doctor came out and said, "Linda, you have to think of your health and your family's health, this is a good decision." We walked in the room together, and he said, "Your Dad and I had a nice talk." He excused himself and Dad said, "Were you crying?" "Yes, Dad." "Because of what the doctor told me?" "Yes, Dad." "Linda, don't cry," which, of course, only made me cry again, "I don't mind, it will be fine." We talked a bit on the way home, and truly I think he was relieved and glad that he would be able to be with Mom as often as he wanted. THAT I was glad of for him and for Mom. What an awful day. The date he will go is January 1st. He is busy packing, doing his Dad thing that he has always done, bless him for that sameness and saneness. Love, me.

November 12, 2000 - The Zoo.

It is a drippy day, the air is heavy with that wet feel that comes from snow and rain mixed together. There are drips of this heavy stuff from every eave and tree. It is a waiting period, waiting for snow, the real stuff. There is supposed to be a storm tonight and tomorrow, but it will have a lighter feel to it and be lovely in its newness. I feel heavy inside too.

I visited Mom today by myself. She hasn't changed. She has the same stare, few words, holds on to my hand. Halfway through our visit she pushed out the words, "I'm glad you came," that was it. Perhaps it takes a long time for her to formulate the words in her mind first, but that is what it's like, pushing out the words. I told her I was glad I had come too, and the rest of the time we watched the other ladies. Chirper was chirping and telling Racer that she better watch out or she knew what she would get. Then Caregiver got in the act with Racer and said she better keep moving or she would smack her one. Then Singer got into it with Picker, who was draped over the love seat on Singer. Singer called me over and told me that she thought I should do something about Picker, but then maybe she should stay with her because the others didn't do anything either, or maybe I should go back to farming because I knew how to handle the plow but not how to handle the women. Then she added that she liked talking to me and would talk to me later. In other words, she dismissed me. And Two Timer was busy telling everyone they had to go now. It was a bit of a zoo on the third floor today. For the most part we just sat and held hands and looked about.

January 15, 2001 - A sad but uncertain tale from the third floor.

It has been a long time in not writing. We have been busy getting Dad moved to the nursing home, and they have worked it so he can be on the third floor with her. So, rooms and beds and such have been moved about to accommodate them. Dad was busy trying to get everything just right, and honestly, even though I cried, I could tell he was as happy as a clam. Mom was looking confused most of the time watching him but remained calm and just observed. I have to say Dad was almost giddy.

But before that Christmas has come and gone. I really don't remember too much of this Christmas. We did all the usual things, but Mom was missing, and Dad was looking toward his move. I hope that Don and the kids had a good time. I must have but don't remember it.

And here it is another new year. Last night the nursing home called to say that Mom wasn't responding to much of anything. Some other signs they were noticing were leading them to believe that Mom may be dying. I froze. I just had no idea what to do, if I had to do something and if I did have to do something, what? Thankfully, Don said, "Let's go." So, he and I and Donny and Laura went out there. We prayed for her. Of course, Dad was already there. After a while I told Don and the kids to go, and I would stay for a bit longer. I combed her hair and sang hymns to her that I knew were her favorites and some of the lullabies that she sang to us when we were kids. Then when everyone was out of the room, I leaned close to her and told her that it was okay to go home, that she didn't need to worry about any of us, and that Dad would be taken care of. I told her I loved her, and was thankful that she was my mother, and that she lived well, but it was okay to leave.

This morning some of the "signs" are gone, but she is still unresponsive and not eating or drinking anything. There is a call in to the doctor, and so we wait. All of us are wondering if it is just the extra pain medication that is coursing through her system, even though she hasn't had any for about 36 hours, and that it just has her snowed, and until that's gone she will be very out of it. There are all kinds of books on the subject of the dying process, but they really didn't help me now that it was possibly staring me in the face. I will update as I am updated myself.

Dad, in spite of the problems he is having with confusion and paranoia, was calm and seemed to understand what was going on. He stayed until they came and put him to bed. I left him there this morning after my visit. My heart says, no, not now, more time, but compassion says, for her sake take her home, Lord. Be with us, Oh, Lord.

January 22, 2001

On January 20th, 2001 Mom passed away peacefully.

January 23, 2001

Time ceased to exist for a few days, at least time as we know it normally. I feel a desire to write and yet how does one start? To say that our time was rich together doesn't even quite say it all. Don, Susan, George, Gina, Gina's youngest child, Dave and Renee, Jay, Laura and Donny, Dad and myself were all with Mom for most of the three days preceding her death. I cannot begin to tell you how thankful I am that they all got here so quickly, and it was not a short travel time. I needed them all, and I know they all needed to be here.

Some of our special friends from Hospice came over and spent time with us as we sat with Mom. The music therapist played his guitar while we sang many of the songs Mom liked. Singer sang the Our Father along with us, and she didn't miss any of the words. We sat for a time and shared our stories and our memories with Mom, with Dad, with each other, and with those who were there from Hospice. Then we sang Ave Maria for Dad since it was his favorite. Mom's eyes were open, and she was looking at one or the other of us, but there was no response, no smile, just looking at our faces.

During the hours and days that we spent in Mom's room, there was a parade of patients rolling their wheelchairs down past her room. Caregiver came in and wanted to make sure Mom was covered up and warm. One of the nurses came in on her day off to say goodbye again. She ministered to us briefly before she left. Jude would tear up each time he would come to take care of Mom and reposition her. Usually Susan and I left, but on one occasion we stayed and were moved at the tenderness with which he cared for Mom. When he was done, he patted her head and said, "Oh, Laura Mae," with such sadness. Many of the nurses and aides came and checked in on her throughout these days and nights. They were very caring of our family as well, and in spite of their obvious care for Mom, they were most respectful of our family time and didn't intrude until such time when we had to take a break and go home. We very much appreciate their respect for us.

Mom died peacefully with all of us there. She died at 11:40 p.m. I am in awe again at our wonderfully created bodies and the tenacity with which we cling to life. Though the last day she was not aware of us visually, we are trusting she knew we were there and heard us as we spoke to her. What a blessing and a gift to us to be able to aid, in any way, our mother, our father's wife, our children's grandmother, my husband's mother-in-law's passing from this life to Jesus and her final home. With love.

January 25, 2001 - Epilogue. On the second floor.

They moved Dad to the second floor because they needed his room on the third floor, and he is more independent than the ladies on the third floor. Dad is doing the best he knows how. He has one of those alarms on his ankle, and he tells me that some thing keeps humming him on his foot. He knows it's there but forgets in the next instant. He says that they must have to put it on me. He cannot find his room most of the time. He has to look at all the names, and then if his roommate is in the room he uses the bathroom down the hall. I think he is leery of the roommate, he is a large man who speaks in a gruff voice. Dad is lost, but trying, and that's all one can ask for. He looked at me yesterday and said, "Linda, I saw Mom at the table at dinner, she was eyeing me. You would have seen her too if you were there." Perhaps Mom is calling to him, surely she is waiting for him, I wouldn't be surprised.

January 27, 2001 - A tale from the lunchroom.

We had a little visit with Dad. He was asleep by the bird cage in the dayroom, sound asleep. Even after we said hello, he didn't want to get up, but he was hungry, and it was time for lunch. We went downstairs with him and got him seated. He got busy putting the bib on himself and one on the table to put his plate on. He fussed and fussed around and then told me that Mom would come down pretty soon, that she would eat all of her food, and that I would see her soon. What could I answer? He either sees her, or he just doesn't remember that she isn't there. He misses her, that I know.

I stopped on the way out to see Singer, and when I asked her how she was, she said, "I'm not alive, I wish they would just let me sleep and then take me to the cemetery." I visited briefly with the other ladies on the third floor. It is difficult to see them. I so miss Mom. Love, me

January 31, 2001 - A happy tale from the second floor.

Dad's 86th birthday is today and what a day. He had a doctor's appointment, which went well, and then as we were coming back into the nursing home one of the nurses said, "Come on, Norm, we have to go into the dining room." When we arrived there, one of Dad's favorite aides started singing Happy Birthday in a very thick Russian accent. I almost expected him to do that Russian dance, he was really belting it out, and Dad loved it! He just beamed. I had brought a cake for Dad. When the singing and the hugging was over Dad enjoyed his piece of cake and the attention, blushing the whole time.

February 2001 - A tale and an end.

They have moved Dad to the third floor. He has a room at the end of the hallway where he and Mom sat so often. It is full of pictures and things that are of he and Mom. I have started to type updates to all of you about Dad, and I can't do it. I don't feel comfortable writing about Dad as I did about Mom. I could tell you many tales and introduce you to all the new people, but Dad's dementia is so sad for me, so full of paranoia and hallucinations that it just seems like an invasion of privacy. I will tell you that he does well, he is busy helping out everyone, even when they don't want it. He said to me the other day that he hoped he was doing a good job there at the nursing home, and I said, "Dad, you are doing a great job!"

Know that I will go faithfully and listen to him, laugh with him, walk with him, care for him and love him, as best I can.

Dad passed away September 25th, 2001, 8 months after his beloved wife.

Rest in peace, Mom and Dad, we love you.

Love, me.

BEHIND WILD EYES STIRS THE HEART
OF A SOUL THAT WAS ONCE BURNING
BRIGHT WITH A MIND THAT WAS
WHOLE.

BEHIND WILD EYES TUCKED AWAY
FAR BENEATH STIRS THE MEMORIES
STRUGGLING, THE MIND WILL NOT
KEEP.

BEHIND WILD EYES LIVES A CRUEL
DISEASE THAT WILL ROB MIND FROM
SOUL WHILE IGNORING ALL PLEAS.

BEHIND WILD EYES IT'S THE SOUL THE
HEART KEEPS, AND THE MEMORIES LIE
STILL BEHIND MIND FAST ASLEEP.

BEHIND WILD EYES HER SOUL PRAYS
FOR THE DAY THAT THE GOOD LORD
WILL TAKE ALL THIS SUFFERING AWAY.

BEHIND WILD EYES IS A SOUL THAT
LIES DEEP WHEN RELEASED FROM THE
BONDAGE THE MIND CANNOT KEEP.

BEHIND WILD EYES THERE'S A CHILD, A
GIRL, A WOMAN, A MOTHER, A WIFE, A
PEARL.

BEHIND WILD EYES STIRS MY
GRANDMOTHER DEAR FOR WITHOUT
HER I KNOW THAT I WOULD NOT BE
HERE.

Linda Todd lives in Marietta, Georgia with her husband and their youngest daughter. She has been blessed with five children, seven step-children and eight grandchildren, so far.

LaVergne, TN USA
23 April 2010
180273LV00001B/29/P